ON THE DEATH OF JEWS

ON THE DEATH OF JEWS

Photographs and History

Nadine Fresco

Translated by Sarah Clift

Published in association with the
United States Holocaust Memorial Museum

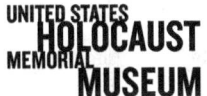

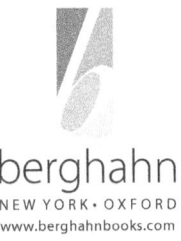

berghahn
NEW YORK · OXFORD
www.berghahnbooks.com

Published in 2021 by
Berghahn Books
www.berghahnbooks.com

English-language edition
© 2021 United States Holocaust Memorial Museum

The assertions, arguments, and conclusions contained herein are those of the author or other contributors. They do not necessarily reflect the opinions of the United States Holocaust Memorial Museum.

French-language edition
"Photographies" in *La mort des juifs*
© Editions du Seuil, 2008
Collection *La Librairie du XXIe siècle*, sous la direction de Maurice Olender.

Photographs on pages xxvii–xxxiv courtesy USHMM and the Zentrale Stelle der Landesjustizverwaltungen (Bundesarchiv-Aussenstelle):

B 162 Bild-02612
B 162 Bild-02614
B 162 Bild-02615
B 162 Bild-02620
B 162 Bild-02621
B 162 Bild-03234
B 162 Bild-02622
B 162 Bild-02623

All rights reserved. Except for the quotation of short passages for the purposes of criticism and review, no part of this book may be reproduced in any form or by any means, electronic or mechanical, including photocopying, recording, or any information storage and retrieval system now known or to be invented, without written permission of the publisher.

Library of Congress Cataloging-in-Publication Data

Names: Fresco, Nadine, author. | Clift, Sarah, translator.
Title: On the Death of Jews: Photographs and History / Nadine Fresco; translated by Sarah Clift.
Other titles: Mort des juifs. Selections. English
Description: New York: Berghahn Books, 2021. | Originally published as a chapter in La mort des juifs. Paris: Seuil, 2008. | Includes bibliographical references and index.
Identifiers: LCCN 2020056063 (print) | LCCN 2020056064 (ebook) | ISBN 9781789208818 (hardback) | ISBN 9781789209242 (paperback) | ISBN 9781789208825 (ebook)
Subjects: LCSH: Holocaust, Jewish (1939–1945)—Latvia—Liepāja—Pictorial works. | Jews—Latvia—Liepāja—Pictorial works. | Massacres—Latvia—Liepāja—Pictorial works.
Classification: LCC DS135.L33 F7513 2021(print) | LCC DS135.L33(ebook) | DDC 940.53/1844—dc23
LC record available at https://lccn.loc.gov/2020056063
LC ebook record available at https://lccn.loc.gov/2020056064

British Library Cataloguing in Publication Data
A catalogue record for this book is available from the British Library

ISBN 978-1-78920-881-8 hardback
ISBN 978-1-78920-924-2 paperback
ISBN 978-1-78920-882-5 ebook

CONTENTS

List of Illustrations	vi
Foreword *Dorota Glowacka*	vii
List of Abbreviations	xxiv
On the Death of Jews	1
Select Bibliography	99

ILLUSTRATIONS

Figures 1 and 2. German civilians watch as the furnishings of the synagogue in Mosbach (Baden-Württemberg) are burned in the town's market square, 10 November 1938.   13

Figure 3. Jews from Lörrach and surroundings (Baden-Württemberg) are about to be herded onto trucks and then taken to deportation trains.   17

Figure 4. German Jews from Coesfeld (North Rhine-Westphalia) are rounded up for deportation to Riga, Latvia, 10 December 1941.   29

Figures 5 and 6. 1941 or 1942, near Orel (220 miles south of Moscow). German soldiers, members of a Propaganda Kompanie, take photographs of three Russian partisans who have been hanged. The placard around the woman's neck reads (in Russian): "This is how partisans end."   31

Figure 7. *Kurzemes Vārds*, 13 December 1941.   47

FOREWORD

Dorota Glowacka

Try to look. Just try and see.
—Charlotte Delbo, *None of Us Will Return*

Charlotte Delbo penned her memoir *None of Us Will Return* to commemorate 230 women with whom she had been transported from Drancy to Auschwitz-Birkenau on 24 January 1943. As one of only forty-nine members of the convoy who had "returned," most of them French political prisoners, Delbo made a commitment to preserve the memory of her martyred comrades. With the images of tortured and dying women indelibly seared in her mind, her narrative is punctuated with the refrain, "Try to look. Just try and see" (*Essayez de regarder. Essayez pour voir*).[1] Delbo's compassionate desire to see transforms her descriptions of horror and humiliation into a work of mourning and into an injunction that those who come after bear witness to what happened to her friends.

Nowhere has similar commitment to an ethics of testimonial gaze been expressed with more lucidity, eloquence, and passion than in *On the Death of Jews*. Straddling the boundary between historical inquiry and personal reflection, this extraordinary text unfolds as a series of encounters with eponymic Holocaust photographs. Although only a small number of photographs are reproduced here, Fresco provides evocative descriptions of many well-known images: synagogues and Torah scrolls burning on the night of *Kristallnacht*; deportations to the ghettos and the camps; and, finally, mass executions in the killing fields of Eastern Europe. The unique set of photographs included in *On the Death of Jews* shows groups of women and children from Liepaja (Liepāja), shortly before they were killed in December 1941 in the dunes of Shkede (Šķēde) on the Baltic Sea. In the last photograph of the series, we see the victims' bodies tumbling into the pit.

The thriving Jewish community of Liepaja, a city in Latvia also known by its German name "Libau," was mainly destroyed between July and December 1941. In an earlier essay titled "Remembering the Unknown," Fresco wrote, "What the Nazis had annihilated over and above individuals, was the very substance of a world, a culture, a history, a way of life"—and for Liepaja these words ring especially true.[2]

Founded in 1625, the town of Liepaja, perched on the shores of the Baltic Sea, was an important hub on merchants' routes, first in German Courland (Kurzeme, in Latvian) and then in tsarist Russia after the region was annexed in 1795.[3] Although Jewish merchants had passed through Liepaja already in the seventeenth century, the records of the first Jewish community date back to 1799. In the mid-1930s, more than seven thousand Jews lived there, tightly woven into the city's rich and diverse social fabric—this was their home. In an interview given to the Shoah Foundation in 1996, Shoshana Kahn, a survivor from Liepaja, reminisced about the city's beauty and the smell of linden trees, which had given the city its name (from *liepa*, the Latvian word for "linden"; the city's coat of arms displays a lion leaning on a linden tree). As elsewhere in Latvia, which had become an independent republic in 1918, Jews in Liepaja enjoyed full autonomy. The community was diverse, bustling with myriad cultural and business activities, as well as with scholarly and religious life. Many of the city's doctors, lawyers, and business owners were Jewish. Kahn recalls, "The Jews [in Liepaja] tried to identify with the higher culture. And in Libau, German was the culture."[4] But, aside from so-called Courland Jews, assimilated to German culture, there were also Yiddish-speaking Jews and some who primarily spoke Russian. As Max Kaufmann, survivor from Riga, recollects in *Churbn Lettland*, his memoir written shortly after the war, Latvian Jews were rabbis and world-renowned secular scholars; painters, musicians, and writers; bank owners and dentists—all of whom played a central role in Latvia's cultural, social, and economic life.[5]

The rise of Latvian ethnonationalism in the 1930s, under the dictatorship of Kārlis Ulmanis, augured the eclipse of the golden era of Latvian Jewry. Ulmanis's ambitions for an independent state were cut short, however, when the Red Army marched into Latvia on 17 June 1940. Immediately, property was confiscated and businesses were nationalized, with thousands of members of the "bourgeoisie" arrested and deported to Siberia. The number of Jews among the deportees was disproportionately high, which did not prevent their Latvian neighbors from blaming them for the evils of communism. As Bernhard Press, another survivor from Riga, bitterly remarked, "The fact that the victims of the KGB also included numerous Jews did not concern the anti-Semites."[6]

At the same time, rumors about the persecution and murder of Jews in Germany and Austria began to reach the Jewish communities in Latvia. George Schwab, a survivor from Liepaja, remembers overhearing rumors that Jewish women in Vienna were forced to use their furs to polish Germans' cars. In his recollection, however, "everyone felt safe in the Baltics. We felt safe. Nothing is going to happen to us."[7] It was a false sense of security, of course. Operation Barbarossa stormed into the Baltic republics at the end of June 1941, and Liepaja, after a five-day siege, was the first city to come under German occupation.[8] The Jews of Liepaja were subjected to a rapid succession of restrictions. Schwab says that he will never forget the humiliation of running into a Latvian classmate on the street and being forced to walk in the gutter: "She sort of looked away, and I felt embarrassed that I was a Jew, that I had to wear this [the yellow star] and I could not go on the sidewalk."[9] Many Latvians greeted Germans as liberators; Kaufmann remembers that on the first day of the occupation, the Latvian hymn was played alongside the Horst Wessel song. Soon, Latvian auxiliary security police would play a major role in arrests, round-ups, and killings. Based in Riga, the infamous Arājs Kommando, named after its leader Viktors Arājs, would travel to the execution sites in blue buses, the sight of which has been carved in the memory of the survivors of the Riga ghetto: "The blue buses drove back and forth."[10] Survivors of the ghetto also recall acts of humiliation against elderly Jewish men, brutal sexual assaults of young Jewish women, and systematic destruction of cultural and religious landmarks. Even the Jewish cemeteries in Riga were obliterated to erase the traces of the city's Jewish past.

The first ghettos in Latvia were established in July 1941, and the Jews of Riga were relocated to the ghetto in September: "One must imagine this move to be roughly similar to the Jews' exodus from Egypt," writes Kaufmann,[11] trying to make sense of the precipitate collapse of the Jewish world. The Riga ghetto was sealed in October: as it turned out, the ghettos mainly served the purpose of concentrating undesirable populations in preparation for mass killings. The majority of Riga Jews were murdered in two large *Aktionen* in the Rumbula forest, just outside the city, on 30 November and 8–9 December 1941. With the ghetto emptied out, thousands of Jews from Czechoslovakia, Austria, and Germany were resettled in the abandoned apartments.[12] Gertrude Schneider, who had been one of these deportees, later remembered that "the new arrivals found food, frozen solid, still on plates."[13]

In Liepaja, mass executions started early in July 1941, escalating when Untersturmführer Wolfgang Kügler took over as SD and Security Police Chief and recruited the help of the Kriegsmarine (War Navy) and the Arājs SD Kommando. Daily executions took place in the Rainis city park, at the Fishermen's Harbor near the Baka lighthouse, and on the beach near the harbor.[14] The victims were killed in small groups to conceal the nature of the operations and to maintain order. In September, a new killing site was established at the former Latvian army shooting range at Shkede, located on the Baltic shore about fifteen kilometers north of the city. Here, on the orders of the new commander of the region, SS General Friedrich Jeckeln, the "final solution" of Liepaja Jews was carried out: 2,749 women, children, and elderly men were shot over the pits in the dunes of Shkede between 15 and 17 December 1941.[15] The annihilation of Liepaja's Jews followed what we now know was a typical pattern of genocide: men of fighting age and male leaders of the community were the first to be rounded up and killed, followed by the root-and-branch murder of women and children.[16] In a short film of the executions carried out at the end of July 1941, we see only men being shot. Photographs of the December executions in Shkede, however, which marked the final stages of the extermination campaign, show women and children.

On 1 July 1942, the remaining Liepaja Jews, 832 in number, were relocated to a small ghetto, the size of one square city block, and forced to perform basic services for the Germans. Among the survivors were George Schwab, who was twelve years old at the time, and his mother; the kommandant of the ghetto, Franz Kerscher, hired Schwab as his errand boy. In October 1943, the ghetto was liquidated and the prisoners were transported to Riga's Kaiserwald concentration camp—which, as Schwab recalls, "was hell ... with constant beatings and screamings."[17] As the Red Army was approaching in October 1944, those still alive in Kaiserwald were transported by ship or rail to Stutthoff concentration camp. With the imminent end of the Third Reich in April 1945, the survivors were put on barges and left adrift at sea without food or drinking water. George Schwab recalls that they were eventually rescued by Norwegian prisoners, but some, including eight survivors from Liepaja, were shot by German navy servicemen as they were wading to the safety of the shore. George Schwab was among a handful who were liberated by the British army a few hours later. Fewer than two hundred Liepaja Jews survived the war, including those who were hidden by Latvian neighbors.[18] As Kaufmann wrote in 1947, expressing his grief, "Jewish Liepaja exists no longer."[19]

After years of searching the archives and mining survivor testimonies, American scholar Edward Anders (a survivor from Liepaja, born E. Alperovitch) and Juris Dubrovskis (a scholar from Riga) compiled a database of 7,142 names of victims and survivors from Liepaja; for almost every murdered Jew of Liepaja, we now have a name.[20] On 4 June 2005, the monument to the victims of the December mass killings was dedicated in Shkede. Designed by sculptor Raimonds Gabaliņš, the monument takes the form of a large menorah, laid out alongside what is believed to be the site of a mass grave.[21] Concluding the dedication ceremony, George Schwab stated, "I hope you look at [this monument] and remember."[22] When the visitors to the memorial turn to look at the Baltic's rolling waves, what they see is likely the last view the condemned saw before they were shot.

The frothing waves can be clearly recognized in the photographs of the executions, taken, most likely, by Carl (Karl)-Emil

Strott, who was stationed in Liepaja between July 1941 and January 1945.²³ Schwab remembers Strott's visits to his parents' apartment: the SS Oberscharführer scavenged for valuables, and one of the prized possessions he took was a stamp collection that belonged to Schwab's brother. The family also owned two Leica cameras: one of them had to be given to a Latvian collaborator, likely a member of the Arājs Kommando, and the other was stolen by the SS Scharführer Erich Handke, who, like Strott, was an avid photographer and one of the officers participating in the *Aktion* at Shkede.²⁴ Although the pictures at Shkede were captured with a Minox camera, I wonder what scenes Handke may have captured looking through the lens of the camera that used to belong to a Jewish family.

A man whose life had been spared because his skills as an electrician were "essential" to the Germans stationed in Liepaja found the negatives of the photographs in Strott's apartment. The photographs were entered as evidence during the *Einsatzgruppen* trials in Berlin and Hannover in 1971. In this volume, Fresco introduces Strott as the man who "saw nothing."²⁵ In his deposition in the 1964 trial of another perpetrator, Strott denied that he had taken the photographs. Although he admitted to having been at the site of the execution, he described his duties as making sure that there were no German or local spectators, so that no one—apparently not even he himself—could "see" anything at all. What Strott presented before the court was a narrative of blindness and willed amnesia.

Another notorious perpetrator with a camera stationed in Liepaja was Reinhard Wiener, a member of the Kriegsmarine who filmed the executions at the end of July 1941.²⁶ Compared to Strott, he was a less reluctant witness: in 1981 he agreed to be interviewed about his film in Tel Aviv, perhaps in pursuit of a perverse claim to fame as the author of the only such extant documentary. It is clear from his interview, however, that he also remained blind to what was unfolding before his camera, even if he could see it clearly. When asked what exactly he had seen, he replied, "I couldn't observe what exactly was going on around when I was filming because I was looking through the lens and I could only see that section that I was looking at through the lens."²⁷ The camera's lens refracted the spectacle, apparently shielding the photographer from the realization that he was participating in mass murder. The presence of the camera also protected him from the emotional impact of what he saw. Thus, while we have evidence that alcohol was often used to alleviate perpetrators' stress and lessen inhibitions, it appears that cameras functioned as buffers that kept the grisly reality of their involvement in genocide at bay. A camera could shrink the photographer's or filmmaker's field of vision to a carefully selected fragment, perhaps giving him an illusion of being in control of what must have eluded his comprehension.

In the interval between Wiener's filming of the killings in Liepaja and Strott's taking the photos at Shkede, the restrictions against photographing executions came into effect; hence, while Wiener described the presence of rows of spectators, the executions in December were hidden from public view. Until the policy was reversed, however, the soldiers were ordered to attend the executions, although evidently many were eager to do so. As the head of the 2nd company of Reserve Police Battalion 13 testified, "The execution area [near the naval port in Liepaja] was visited by scores of German spectators from the Navy and the Reichsbahn (state railway). I turned to Kügler and said in no uncertain terms that it was intolerable that shootings were carried out in front of spectators."[28] In his interview, Wiener recalled that obtaining permission to film was easy, and even after prohibitions against filming executions were introduced, no real measures were undertaken to confiscate the existing footage. In fact, cases of courts-martial for disobeying the prohibition were rare. Although, during the trial of SS-Untersturmführer Max Täubner in May 1943, "his disobedience on account of taking photographs [was] viewed as a particularly serious case," an equally damning circumstance was the fact that he had tried to coerce his wife into having an abortion, in violation of the Nazi policies of population control. In any case, Täubner received a lenient sentence of five years' imprisonment, and he was promptly pardoned in January 1945.[29]

During the campaign in the East, German soldiers made excellent use of small-size cameras (Minox, Zeiss Icon, and a more expensive Leica) that could easily fit into a backpack or even a pocket. They took thousands of photographs, many of which were discovered after the war, although only some later became iconic, circulating in documentary films, visual histories of the Holocaust, and museum exhibits. For the soldiers, these photographs were prized possessions, collected in albums, shared among their comrades, and sent home as "mementos," as if "shooting" the destruction of the Jewish communities had been necessary to make the vision of Germany's *Volkskörper* (national body), cleansed of the Jewish presence, real.

On the Death of Jews recounts the fate of the destroyed Jewish communities, but it also offers a visual anamnesis of the history that the Nazi regime sought to remake in their own image. One of the most striking episodes early in the book is Fresco's description of the photograph that shows the citizens of the town of Mosbach assembled in the market square on 10 November 1938 to watch the burning of the furniture from a nearby synagogue. The onlookers are arranged several rows deep.[30] Another picture shows the synagogue veiled in thick smoke. Throughout her commentary on this photograph, and then continuing for the remainder of the book, Fresco repeats the phrase *"vor aller Augen"* (before everyone's eyes) as if it were an incantation. This reiterated phrase amplifies the violence of the spectators' gaze and enhances the effect of this scene as a gruesome, carnivalesque ritual. Yet, Fresco's inference that the fabric flung on top of the heap of furniture was probably the covers of the Holy Ark suddenly conjures a very different point of view: namely, survivors' recollections of cultural destruction. Helga Franks, who was ten years old in November 1938, was on her way to school located in a Berlin synagogue when she saw that the building was "lit up," and the firemen with hoses were standing around, protecting the nearby houses: "I went back to the apartment and I was crying. The synagogue was burning!"[31] Three years later, standing on the balcony of his house in Riga, Kaufmann saw "the burning of the great synagogue on Gogol Street and the Old-New Synagogue and the Hasidic houses of prayer [in Riga]. Many Jews, dressed in their prayer shawls and *talith* [sic], flung themselves into the flames to save the Torahs," bringing to mind apocalyptic scenes from Marc Chagall's paintings.[32]

In another remarkable passage, Fresco describes a photograph that shows the deportation of a group of Jewish inhabitants of "a small town in the Rhineland."[33] She remarks on the professional quality of the shot, but then she redirects our attention to the faces of the deportees. The final destination of this transport will be Riga, Latvia, the city to which thousands of German and Austrian Jews were deported.[34] Although this photograph was also intended as part of Nazi propaganda, Fresco's description submits it to a double retake: she inscribes the fate of the Jews of Mosbach into the history of this German city, from which it was efficiently airbrushed after the war, as if forcing the photograph to say, *J'accuse!* At the same time, by focusing the reader's gaze on a group of condemned individuals, she resignifies this image as a work of mourning.

In her book *On Photography*, Susan Sontag, who would never forget the shock of seeing, at age twelve, the photographs of the liberation of the camps, draws attention to the violence inherent in the act of photographing: the camera, she writes, is a phallic, predatory weapon, while the act of taking pictures is "a semblance of appropriation, a semblance of rape."[35] In the context of Holocaust photographs, this violence is literalized: at the sites of mass executions, the clicking of the shutter reverberates with the salvos of guns, the coalescence brought out when a more neutral French word, *les clichés,* is translated as "shots." Similarly, looking at the well-known photograph of the four women and the girl shortly before their execution at Shkede (see this book's cover), Marianne Hirsch comments: "Displayed in their full vulnerability and humiliation they are doubly exposed in their nakedness and their powerlessness. They are shot before they are shot."[36] Fresco notes, "Only the youngest women, it seems, were made to strip naked," drawing attention to the prurient nature of the camera's gaze.[37] It is no coincidence that many of the iconic Holocaust photographs show violated and naked female bodies.[38] Yet, looking at the same photographs, Shoshana Kahn sees a friend rather than a degraded emblem of Nazi atrocities: "Those are people from my—there is a girl from my class. She sits like that . . . Jenny Brun. She sits like that, naked in the ice."[39] Kahn looks at this tortured likeness of Jenny with compassion, as if deflecting the murderous, sexualized Nazi gaze away from her former classmate's body.

That these photographs exist, writes Fresco, is testimony that the persecution and murder of the Jews "had its witnesses, at the same time as it had its victims and its perpetrators."⁴⁰ The presence of a photographer can be traced in the trajectory of his gaze as he calibrated the best shot; although he is invisible, his gestures are imprinted in the posture and facial expressions of those whom he captured in the picture. In the photographs described by Fresco, there are also numerous bystanders present at the scene, some caught on camera and others cropped just outside the frame.

According to French philosopher Emmanuel Lévinas, we are all primarily witnesses to the lives and the suffering of others: "The subject in which the other is in the same . . . bears witness to it."⁴¹ Through these acts of witnessing, we are ethically bound to others, for whom we are responsible and whose lives and well-being are inseparable from ours. This undeclinable ethical duty does not render murder and betrayal of the other impossible, as Lévinas, a Holocaust survivor originally from Kaunas, Lithuania, knew well. Yet, because we are always implicated in the lives of others, even if we turn away from the spectacle of their suffering, we are witnesses nevertheless—albeit, perhaps unwilling or even hostile ones who refuse to see the other's face. A woman with a child in her arms gawking at a Jewish man having his beard cut off (I am thinking of a well-known image from the Warsaw ghetto), the onlookers assembled in the market square in Mosbach, and Strott standing behind the camera in Shkede are negative witnesses—witnesses in spite of themselves. Within the purview of Lévinas's ethics, even a murderer (and, at his trial, Carl-Emil Strott was found guilty of murder) bears witness to the lives he has helped extinguish, although he is a reluctant, self-incriminating, and "unseeing" witness. Regardless of the murderous intent, writes Lévinas, the other always "concerns me" and "looks at me" (*Il me regarde*).⁴²

What about contemporary witnesses? Looking at the photographs of the executions at Shkede, we have to imagine ourselves standing in the exact place from which they were taken, which is likely identical to the spot from which the shots were fired. As cospectators after the fact, we are implicated in this scene of unspeakable violence unfolding before our eyes: *vor unseren Augen*. Fresco's book demands that we put ourselves in the place of this negative witness so that we can look at the victims depicted in the photographs "otherwise" (to borrow Lévinas' expression signifying primordial responsibility), so that we can "see" them look at us. By orchestrating this imperceptible yet radical shift in the trajectory of the gaze, Fresco coimplicates us in this look, enabling a passage from the perpetrator's negative witnessing to ethical testimony and remembrance. As she reminds us, such testimonial practice of radically disrupting the Nazi gaze was initiated already in 1960 when Gerhard Schoenberner published *Der gelbe Stern* (The Yellow Star), an album of Holocaust photographs, for his "compatriots who did not want to see."[43]

While the debates about Holocaust photographs have revolved around the question of whether images of atrocity desensitize us to horror or, conversely, have the capacity to provoke empathy and awaken our conscience,[44] the fundamental question that Fresco posits is of a different nature altogether. Renowned for her work on antisemitism and Holocaust denial, she focuses on the processes of forgetting, denial, and historical distortion. What she puts in full view in *On the Death of Jews*, however, are the mechanisms that first set in motion the very possibility of denying that "it happened." These mechanisms were, paradoxically perhaps, enabled by the perpetrators' compulsive photographing of the acts of both symbolic and physical destruction of Jewish existence in Europe. But, as Fresco writes in an earlier essay entitled "Negating the Dead," fabricating denial also "reveals the true weight of genocide."[45] This is why it is imperative that we look at the images that have been bequeathed to us by perpetrators from an entirely different angle. Rather than numb us to horror, these photographs, endlessly recycled throughout the postmemorial landscape, can interrupt the complacency of our habits of seeing (and the habits of not seeing). "Through repetition," writes Hirsch, "the postmemorial viewers attempt . . . to re-envision and redirect, the mortifying gaze of these surviving images."[46] If the Nazi gaze was like the deadly look of the Medusa who turned living beings into stone, as Primo Levi famously wrote, we are now reminded that, in the ancient myth, Medusa was a beautiful woman and a beloved daughter before she was violated, turned into a monster, and then decapitated.[47] So were the women in the photographs from Shkede.

Thus, when we look at these images, we must reconceive what "the death of Jews" means, as the title of Fresco's book stipulates. German Jewish thinker Hannah Arendt once wrote that the true force of annihilation in the Nazi camps (and, we must add, in the killing fields of Eastern Europe) was that *"they took away the individual's own death*, proving henceforth nothing belonged to him and he belonged to no one."[48] Fresco's unique engagement with photographs from the Shoah shows that, although we cannot return the victims to the world of the living, perhaps we can at least give them back their deaths. Through careful historical research, we can wrest their deaths from the anonymity of mass destruction and situate them in the context of former Jewish life in Eastern Europe. Indeed, as we have seen, it is largely the rediscovery of the photographs that gave the impetus to the efforts to recreate and commemorate the life of the Jewish community in Liepaja. Looking at the photographs, Fresco pries the Jewish victims' unique lives from the frames into which they were forced by the perpetrators, and she releases them into the current of history and memory. Referring to a group of forty German Jewish refugees who, when they found themselves unwelcome in occupied France, wrote a desperate letter to the prefecture, Fresco writes, "You can almost hear their voices."[49] In *On the Death of Jews*, we can almost see the victims' faces, hidden behind the grimace of terror or a forced pose that was captured by the camera.

Fresco has carefully documented the itineraries that led European Jews to the sites of their murders. In that sense, the Shkede photographs she reproduces are just that: historical documentation. And yet, although the book is entirely devoid of pathos, every word in *On the Death of Jews* is unsettling, as if it were choked with sorrow, just as the photographs, despite their objective status as evidence, are unbearable to look at. The elegiac rhythm of Fresco's narrative brings to mind the tonality of Sarah Kofman's *Paroles suffoquées* (Smothered Words), in which the French philosopher struggles with the tension between the necessity of commemorating her father's death in Auschwitz and the impossibility of "saying it." As a result, Kofman's narrative is written in impossible words: "Knotted words ... which stick in your throat and cause you to suffocate, to lose your breath, which asphyxiate you, taking away the possibility of even beginning."[50] Every paragraph of *On the Death of Jews* is suffused with similar breathlessness.

Intellectual historian Dominick LaCapra has argued for a participatory model of writing history, which would integrate empathy and account for the transferential impact of past traumas on the historian. This modality of "empathic unsettlement" in historical writing would allow for productive, "tense interplay between ... objective reconstruction and affective response to the voice of the victims."[51] Yet even LaCapra's empathic model of "writing history, writing trauma" cannot explain the undercurrent of grief that runs through Fresco's text and that leaves me dumbstruck every time I read it.

In "Remembering the Unknown," Fresco recounts interviews with eight Jewish men and women born shortly after the war in France.[52] The members of the second generation, who inherited "wounds of memory of parents frozen in silence,"[53] are bound together by the absence of the memory of the past that has affected them deeply, the past that holds them in its grip.[54] Silences weighed with that history seep through the pages of Fresco's encounters with Holocaust photographs, the emotion occasionally expressed in a choking succession of sentence fragments: "Refugee. A national. Turned away. Alien, Jew. In France. 'It is right that he should pay'";[55] or in a series of repeated negations: "These photographs do not say. . . . And the little one. . . . whose face we cannot see. . . . We do not hear whether she is crying. Nor do these photographs say whether, as unthinkable as this is. . . ."[56] Suddenly, the refrain *vor aller Augen* returns with the force of traumatic compulsion to repeat. Inflected with grief, it keeps the reader riveted to the sights of displacement and loss. Yet, as Hirsch has argued, although such endless repetition of the image might carry the danger of overidentification with the victim, for the second generation, it also enables the transmission of an inherited traumatic past in such a way that it can be worked through.[57]

Nadine Fresco's book, which I read for the first time almost ten years ago, left me with the images that, to echo Susan Sontag's words, have haunted me ever since;[58] the images that can never fade "out of sight, out of mind." This translation of *On the Death of Jews* into English will make it possible for many new readers to apprehend them outside of their immediate frames and to think about them beyond the accustomed trajectories of Holocaust history; that is, to look at them and try to see.

Dorota Glowacka is Professor of Humanities at the University of Kings' College (Canada). She is the author of *Po tamtej stronie: świadectwo, afekt, wyobraźnia* (2017) and *Disappearing Traces* (2012), and co-editor of *Imaginary Neighbors* (2007) and *Between Ethics and Aesthetics* (2002).

Notes

1. Charlotte Delbo, "None of Us Will Return," in *Auschwitz and After*, trans. Rosette C. Lamont (Boston: Beacon Press, 1968), 95. Delbo, *Aucun de nous ne reviendra* (Paris: Minuit, 1970), 137.
2. Nadine Fresco, "Remembering the Unknown," trans. Alan Sheridan, *International Review of Psycho-Analysis* 11 (1984): 20. The essay was originally published in *Nouvelle Revue de Psychanalyse* 24 (1981).
3. After the annexation, Germans living in the Courland Governorate retained autonomy and privileges.
4. Transcript of Shoshana Kahn interview, USC Shoah Foundation Visual History Archive, interview Code 16106, 3–4.
5. Max Kaufmann, *Churbn Lettland: The Destruction of the Jews of Latvia*, ed. Gertrude Schneider and Erhard Roy Wiehn, trans. Laimdota Mazzarins (Konstanz, Germany: Hartung-Gorre Publishers, 2010 [1947]), 30.
6. Bernhard Press, *The Murder of the Jews in Latvia, 1941–45*, trans. Laimdota Mazzarins (Evanston, IL: Northwestern University Press), 34. See also Press, "A Town Named Libau (Liepaja, Latvia)," www.jewishgen.org/yizkor/libau/libau.html.
7. Transcript of interview with George Schwab, 18 March 2005, USHMM Jeff and Toby Herr Oral History Archive, 2005 RG-50.030*0493, 20.
8. Andrew Ezergailis emphasizes the city's spirit of resistance, which, in his view, was also behind its ethnically Latvian inhabitants' more compassionate attitude toward the Jews than elsewhere in German occupied Latvia. See Andrew Ezergailis, "The Killings in the Cities: Liepaja," in *Jews in Liepaja, Latvia, 1941–45: A Memorial Book*, ed. Edward Anders and Juris Dubrovskis, 1–11 (Burlingame, CA: Anders Press, 2001).
9. Transcript of George Schwab interview, 44.
10. Kaufmann, *Churbn Lettland*, 68.

11. Kaufmann, *Churbn Lettland*, 49.
12. Martin Dean and Geoffrey P. Megargee, eds., "Estonia and Latvia Regions," *The United States Holocaust Memorial Museum Encyclopedia of Camps and Ghettos*, vol. 2 (Bloomington: Indiana University Press in association with the USHMM, 2012), 992–96. See also Josifs Šteimanis, *History of Latvian Jews*, trans. Helena Belova, ed. Edward Anders (New York: Columbia University Press, 2002).
13. Gertrude Schneider, *Journey into Terror: Story of the Riga Ghetto* (New York: Ark House, 1979).
14. Ezergailis, "The Killings in the Cities," 6.
15. Jeckeln was previously in charge of the massacres in Babi Yar, on the outskirts of Kiev, occupied Ukraine, and of the Rumbula killings in Riga.
16. See Adam Jones, "Gendering Genocide," in *Genocide: A Comprehensive Introduction* (New York: Routledge, 2012), 464–98.
17. Transcript of George Schwab interview, 57.
18. 138 Latvians (including 14 from Libau) were declared Righteous among the Nations by Yad Vashem in Israel for helping Jews during the war. See https://www.yadvashem.org/yv/pdf-drupal/latvia.pdf.
19. Kaufmann, *Churbn Lettland*, 162.
20. See Edward Anders and Juris Dubrovskis, "Who Died in the Holocaust? Recovering Names from Official Records," *Holocaust and Genocide Studies* 17, no. 1 (Spring 2003): 114–38.
21. In 1993, the remains of the Jews who had been shot in Rainis Park in July 1941 were reburied in the Liepaja Jewish Cemetery and a granite stone with the Star of David was unveiled. In 2004, a memorial wall was installed next to the memorial, with 6,428 names of the Jews of Liepaja, as well as 46 names of the Latvian rescuers.
22. *Memorial to the Jews of Liepaja (Libau): Victims of the Holocaust (1941–1945)*, DVD 0148, USHMM.
23. See Ezergailis, "The Killings in the Cities," 4.
24. Transcript of George Schwab interview, 42, and a personal conversation with Schwab, 6 July 2019. The information on Handke was obtained at https://www.yadvashem.org/untoldstories/database/murderSite.asp?site_id=572, accessed on 7 July 2019.
25. Fresco, see below, 57. In his own trial in Hannover in 1971, Strott was found guilty of direct participation in the executions, but, as did the other members of the SD tried in Hannover, he got a light prison sentence. See "Liepaja," *Encyclopaedia of Camps and Ghettos*, vol. 2, part B, 1,011–14.
26. Reinhard Wiener, *Juden Exekution in Libau 1941* [Execution of Jews in Liepaja], Steven Spielberg Film and Video Archive, RG Number: RG-60.1767, Film ID: 4149. Also accessible at https://www.youtube.com/watch?v=mroRsZ5ygUY.

27. The interview with Reinhard Wiener was conducted in Tel Aviv on 27 September 1981.
28. Ernst Klee et al, eds.,*"The Good Old Days": The Holocaust as Seen by Its Perpetrators and Bystanders*, trans. Deborah Burnstone (Old Saybrook, CT: Konecky and Konecky, 1991), 128–29.
29. Klee et al, *"The Good Old Days,"* 202.
30. Fresco, see below, 13. See the photograph with the caption "German civilians watch as the furnishings of the synagogue in Mosbach (Baden-Württemberg) are burned in the town's market square."
31. Interview with Helga Franks, the USHMM Jeff and Toby Herr Oral History Archive, 6 August 1991. 1989.346.19 | RG Number: RG-50.031.0019.
32. Kaufmann, *Churbn Lettland*, 39.
33. Fresco, see below, 29.
34. The photograph with the caption indicating the destination of the transport is reproduced in Reinhard Rürup, *Vor aller Augen: Fotodokumente des nationalsozialistischen Terrors in der Provinz / Klaus Hesse und Philipp Springer* (Essen: Klartext, 2002), 153.
35. Susan Sontag, *On Photography* (New York: Farrar, Straus and Giroux, 1977), 24.
36. Marianne Hirsch, "Surviving Images: Holocaust Photographs and the Work of Postmemory," *The Yale Journal of Criticism* 14, no. 1 (2001): 24.
37. Fresco, see below, 51.
38. See also Janina Struk, "Images of Women in Holocaust Photography," *Feminist Review* 88 (2008): 11–21.
39. Interview with Shoshana Kahn, USC Shoah Foundation Visual History Archive, interview Code 16106, transcript, 3–4.
40. Fresco, see below, 9.
41. Emmanuel Lévinas, *Otherwise Than Being or Beyond Essence*, trans. Alphonso Lingis (Pittsburgh: Duquesne University Press, 1998), 146.
42. Emmanuel Lévinas, *God, Death, and Time*, trans. Bettina Bergo (Stanford: Stanford University Press), 196, and *Dieu, la mort et le temps* (Paris: Le Livre de Poche, 2006), 2,001.
43. Fresco, see below, 5.
44. See Barbie Zelizer, *Remembering to Forget: Holocaust Memory through the Camera's Eye* (Chicago: University of Chicago Press, 1998), and Janina Struk, *Photographing the Holocaust: Interpretations of the Evidence* (London: L. B. Tauris, 2004). See also Griselda Pollock, "Photographing Atrocity: Becoming Iconic?" in *Picturing Atrocity: Photography in Crisis*, ed. Geoffrey Patchen et al. (London: Reaktion Books, 2012), and Brad Prager, "On the Liberation of Perpetrator Photography," in *Visualizing the Holocaust: Documents, Aesthetic, Memory*, ed. David Bathrick et al. (Rochester, NY: Camden House, 2008), 19–37.

45. Nadine Fresco, "Negating the Dead," in *Holocaust Remembrance: The Shapes of Memory*, ed. Geoffrey H. Hartman (Oxford: Basil Blackwell, 1994), 191.
46. Hirsch, "Surviving Images," 8.
47. Primo Levi, *The Drowned and the Saved* (2007), 100, and Ovid, *Metapmorphoses*, book IV, trans. Rolfe Humphries (Bloomington: Indiana University Press, 1955), 101–6.
48. Hannah Arendt, *The Origins of Totalitarianism* (New York: Harcourt Brace Jovanovich, 1973), 452; emphasis in original.
49. Fresco, see below, 27.
50. Sarah Kofman, *Smothered Words*, trans. Madelaine Dobie (Evanston, IL: Northwestern University Press, 1998), 39.
51. Dominick LaCapra, *Writing History, Writing Trauma* (Baltimore: Johns Hopkins University Press, 2001), 109.
52. Fresco, "Remembering the Unknown," 417.
53. Fresco, "Remembering the Unknown," 419.
54. Fresco, "Remembering the Unknown," 417. Efraim Sicher speaks of the second generation as bearing "the scar without the wound" in *Breaking the Crystal* (Champaign: University of Illinois Press), 27.
55. Fresco, see below, 24.
56. Fresco, see below, 51.
57. Hirsch, "Surviving Images," 9.
58. Susan Sontag concludes, "Let the atrocity images haunt us. . . . The images say: This is what human beings are capable of doing. . . . Don't forget." Susan Sontag, *Regarding the Pain of Others* (New York: Farrar, Straus and Giroux, 2003), 115.

ABBREVIATIONS

CDJC: Centre de documentation juive contemporaine. Mémorial de la Shoah—Center for Contemporary Jewish Documentation. Shoah Memorial (Paris)

FFDJF: Fils et filles des déportés juifs de France—Sons and Daughters of Jewish Deportees from France

GESTAPO: Geheime Staatspolizei—Secret State Police: Section IV of the RSHA

LVVA: Latvijas Valsts vēstures arhīvs—National Historical Archives of Latvia

MOTLC: Museum of Tolerance. A Simon Wiesenthal Center Museum. Multimedia Learning Center

NSDAP: Nationalsozialistische Deutsche Arbeiterpartei—literally "the National-Socialist Workers' Party of Germany" (the Nazi Party)

RSHA: Reichssicherheitshauptamt—Reich Security Main Office

SA: Sturmabteilung—Storm Detachment

SCHUPO: Schutzpolizei—Protection Police

SS: Schutzstaffel—literally "Protection Squadron" (the Nazi Party's paramilitary forces)

USHMM: The United States Holocaust Memorial Museum

Zentrale Stelle, Ludwigsburg: Zentrale Stelle der Landesjustizverwaltungen zur Aufklärung nationalsozialistischer Verbrechen—Central Office of the State Justice Administrations for the Investigation of National Socialist Crimes, Ludwigsburg, Germany

In memory of my parents

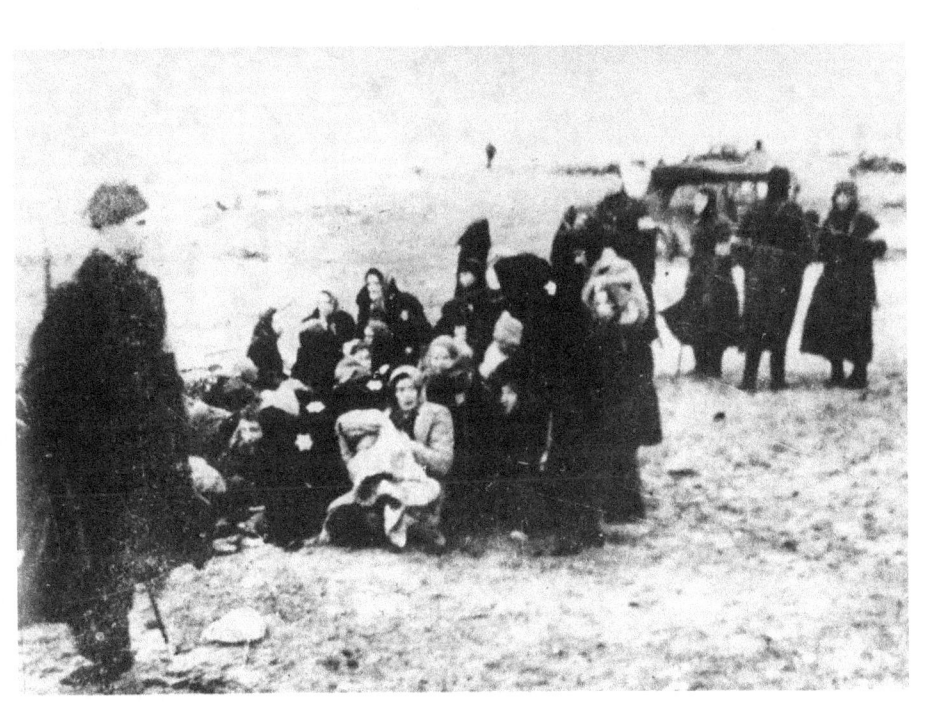

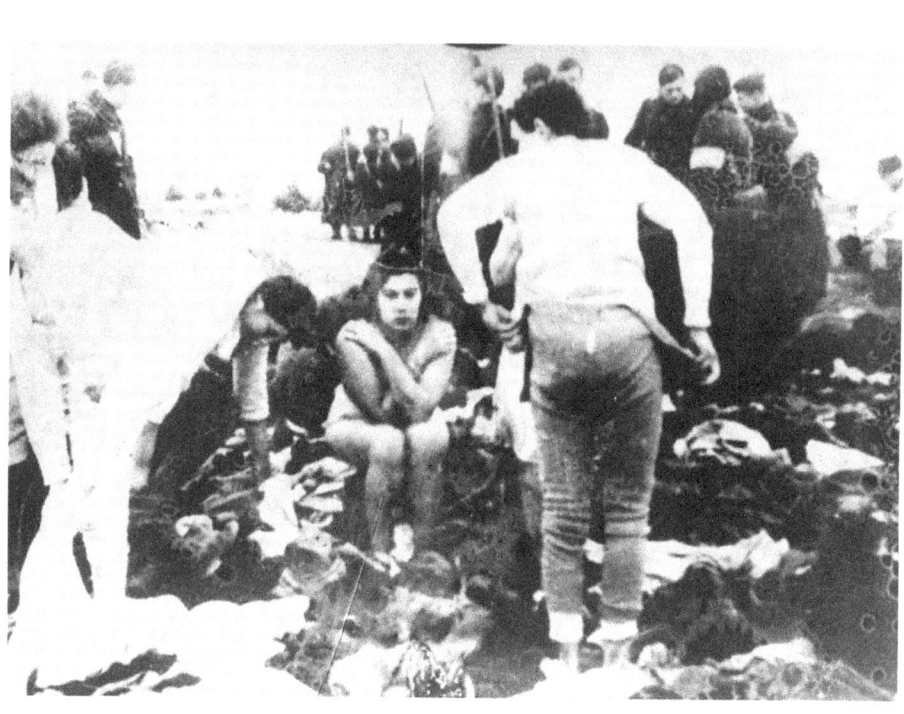

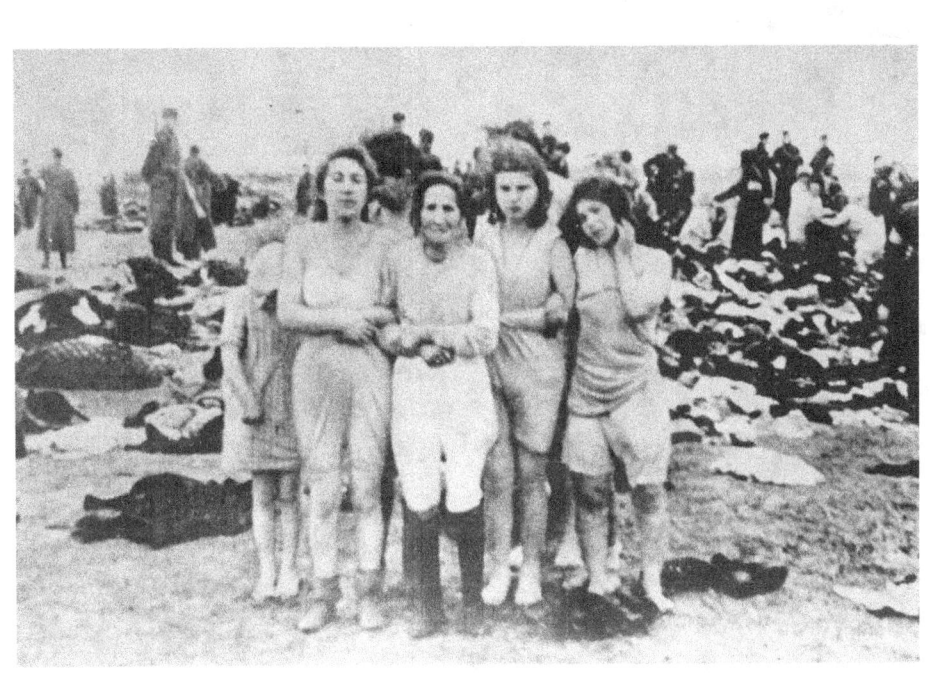

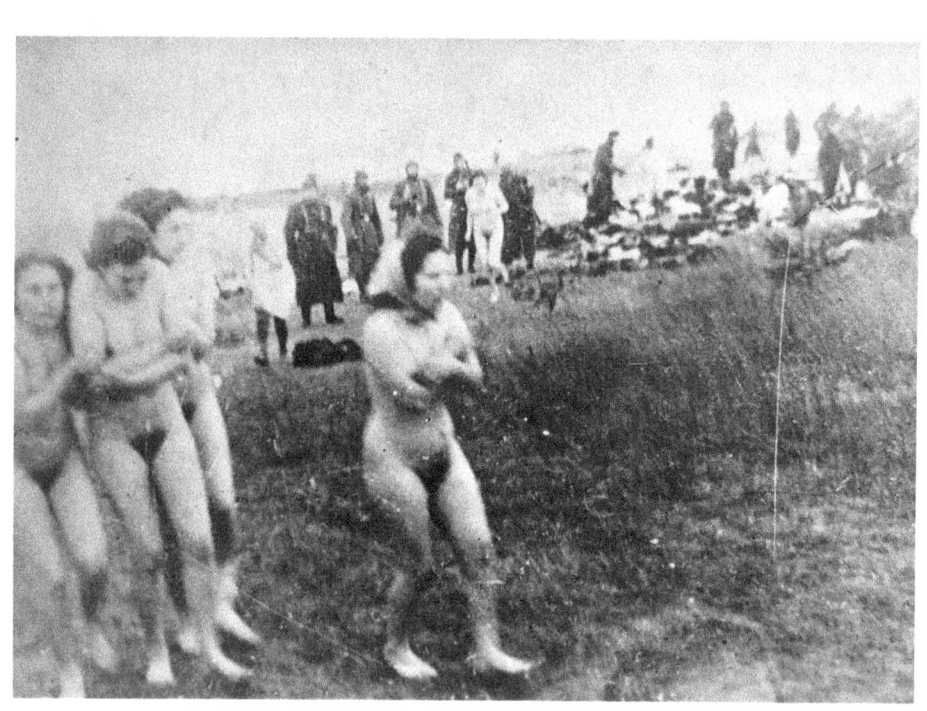

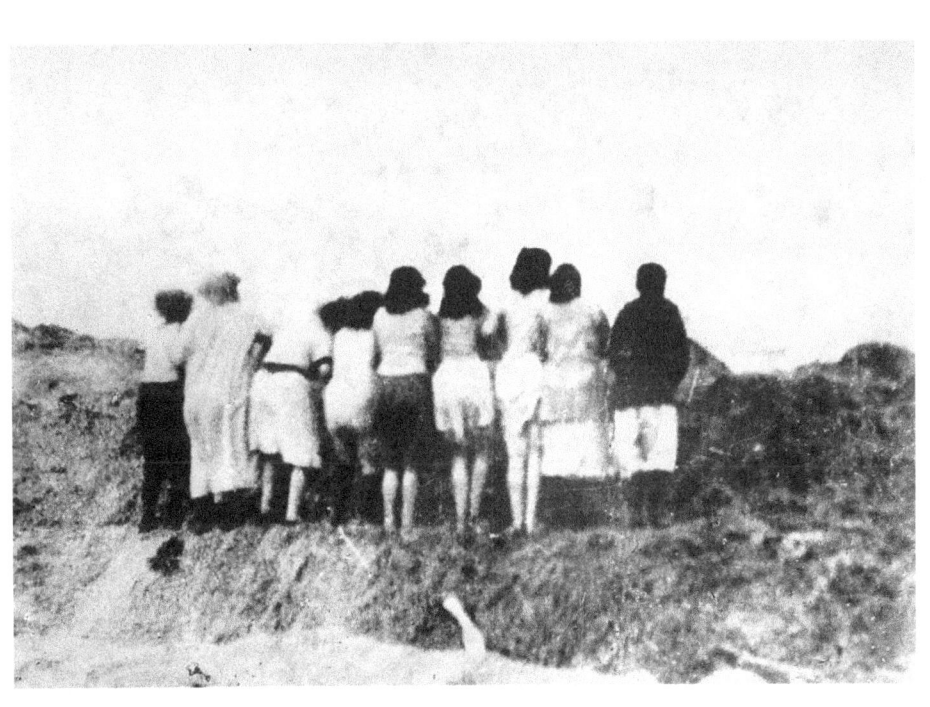

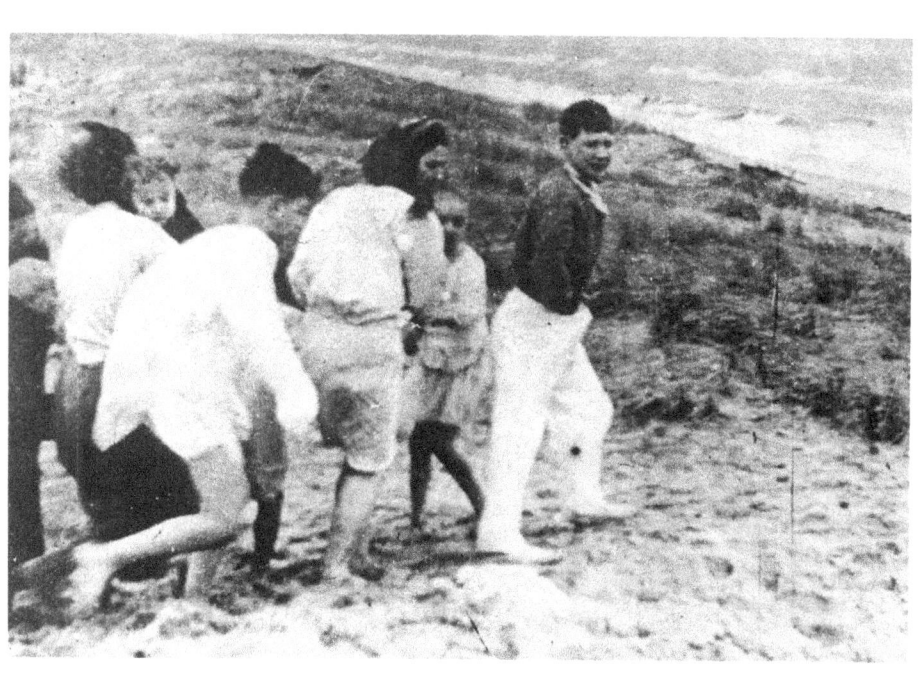

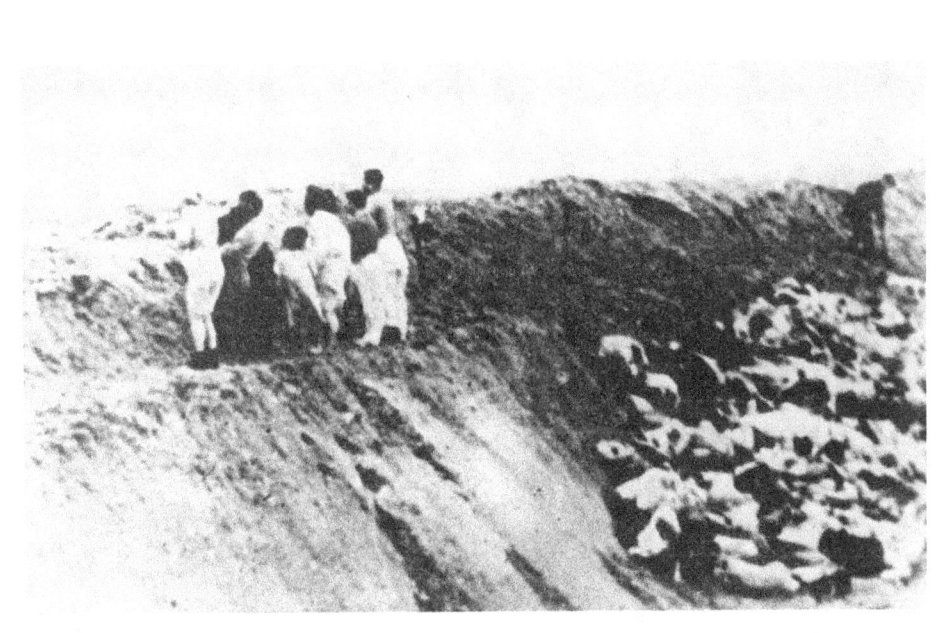

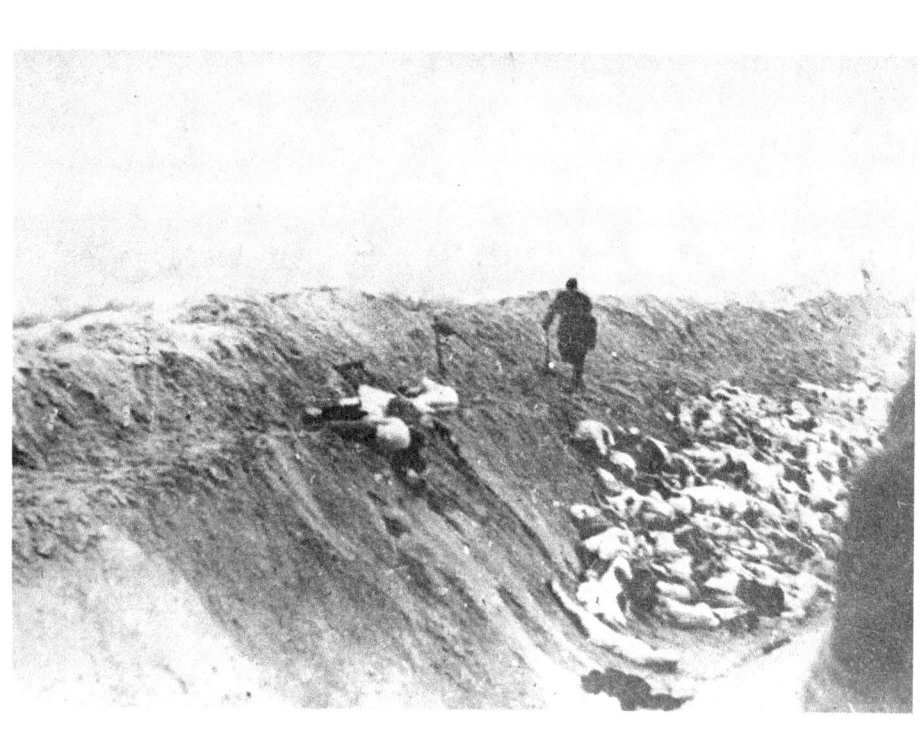

The eight photographs that open this book are among the very few that show the death of Jews at the moment of its execution during the Second World War. Because so few exist, it is these we often see. In books, films, and exhibits, and on websites that deal with this death as it was underway.

To whom do these photographs belong? Who owns the rights to them? And what rights come into play here? Moral right? The *copyright*, a right so widespread that it only needs the laconic but vigilant symbol ©? As soon as such questions are posed, they reveal conflicts of interest that are often as intense as they are dynamic and shifting. These issues have become even more pointed now that history and memory have gone "online": questions involving appropriation are constantly being raised by the Internet. The eight photographs reproduced here illustrate with abundant clarity this mobility of conflicts and the instability of the agreements put in place to shut them down.

In the 1990 edition of *The Pictorial History of the Holocaust*, a book published by the Israeli museum Yad Vashem, these photographs fell under the copyright designation "All photos © Yad Vashem, Jerusalem."[1] For years, some of these shots could be found on the Simon Wiesenthal Center website together with the Center's copyright symbol, after which most of them remained there, but with no copyright designation.[2] Also, six of the eight photographs reproduced here spent years on the United States Holocaust Memorial Museum (USHMM) website under the copyright designation "Copyright: Public Domain." Until one day in July 2008, when they promptly disappeared.[3]

Like other documents, these photographs are not, by virtue of their very existence, protected against identification errors. Some are captioned as coming from elsewhere than the place where the murders they show happened, while others, made elsewhere, are said to have been taken in that place.

Solely by virtue of their existence, these photographs have been no more immune than other documents from shameful exploitations. And there have been plenty of them. The creators of a short-lived Jewish anti-Palestinian website, for instance, insulted the memory of its coreligionists by posting images of their persecuted faces and bodies, including those of the woman and three adolescents advancing naked with arms crossed to shield them from the cold, "in case the Arab world and their oil-thirsty supporters have forgotten what a real Holocaust is."[4]

Alain Resnais's 1956 film *Night and Fog* includes one of these photos.[5] The one with the woman and the three adolescents. Around the twentieth minute of this half-hour long film, we are shown a train full of dead bodies piled on top of one another. The voice-over, written by Jean Cayrol,[6] says, "For some, the selection has already been made. For others, it is made right on the spot. Those on the left will go to work. Those on the right. . . ."[7] These images were taken a few minutes before an extermination." Just as this final phrase is being uttered, a silent sequence of five shots containing five photographs begins—photographs of people who are mostly undressed or already naked a few moments before their extermination. The fourth is that of the woman and the adolescents. Resnais came across some of these photographs in the collections of the Jewish Historical Institute in Warsaw. The fourth he found in Paris in the archives at the Center for Contemporary Jewish Documentation.[8] A series of shots without comment, then. As they say, the images speak for themselves. The commentary starts up again, this time in front of a row of cylinders that have a skull and crossbones on them: "Killing by hand takes time. Cylinders of Zyklon gas are ordered." In 1956, the five photographs that appeared in *Night and Fog* were hardly known, if at all. Hearing the voice-over that precedes and follows these images, at the same time as seeing the buildings of a camp, the viewer thinks that these "few moments" are happening just before the deportees are to be taken to the gas chamber. He does not know that these undressed persons are going to be killed elsewhere, in the open air and by firearm, a few moments later.⁹

American documentary filmmaker Leo Hurwitz is put in charge of the video recording of the hearings for Adolf Eichmann's trial, which begins in Jerusalem on 11 April 1961. At the request of the prosecution to make the presentation of facts "more vivid and concrete," as prosecutor Gideon Hausner puts it, Hurwitz also makes a one-hour long film—a montage consisting of extracts from several documentaries, including *Night and Fog*.¹⁰ This montage is screened on 8 June during a closed session, journalists excepted. The photograph of the woman and the three adolescents is included in this montage. Eichmann sees it on that day for the second time in Jerusalem: days earlier, when court was not in session, they had screened *Night and Fog* for him to watch from the "glass cage" in which, for security reasons, he made his court appearances for the entire duration of the proceedings.¹¹ Leo Hurwitz also films this session during which Eichmann, in a practically empty courtroom, watches the Resnais film in its entirety.¹²

Images *en abyme*. The viewer watches Eichmann watching a film in which he sees the naked woman and adolescents, whose photograph had been taken a few moments before their deaths.

Gerhard Schoenberner, a political science student in West Berlin, is twenty-six years old when he goes to Poland in 1957 with some other German students. They are taking advantage of the "Polish October" atmosphere of the previous year, a sign of the "thaw" that had begun in the Eastern Bloc following Stalin's death. They go to visit Auschwitz then, at a time when such visits are still very rare. Upon their return, these German students are even more aware than they were before the trip of how crucial it is for their compatriots to confront head-on the crimes that had been perpetrated by their country. But the Germany of that time did not want to see, and the elites, having largely collaborated, had also largely succeeded in returning to their former positions. "I do not know anyone my age," reports German writer Lothar Baier (1942–2004), "who learned anything in school about the camps, the SS, the Nazi party, their racial policies, the program to exterminate the Jews. When anyone brought up the period 1933 to 1945, it was to talk about the war. Our teachers, mostly former combatants, substituted a history lesson with stories about their own heroic deeds. The Nazi system was passed over in silence, quite simply because practically all of our teachers had emerged from it."[13] Schoenberner and his friends succeed in organizing an exhibition that opens in the spring of 1960 in West Berlin's Kongresshalle before touring other large West German cities. Entitled "The Past Exhorts: An Exhibit of the History of the Jews and Their Persecution under the Third Reich," it is the first exhibition of its kind in the Federal Republic.[14] During the same period, Schoenberner continues his search for images with the aim of collecting them into a volume, and travels to many centers housing archives. To London, Paris, Warsaw, Amsterdam. To Moscow, too, where, at the State Archives in 1959, as he is sorting through copious boxes filled with photographs—the majority of which were of little interest and poor technical quality—he stumbles upon a "real discovery." A series that he had not seen anywhere up to that point and that had not yet been published anywhere.[15]

The eight photographs reproduced here belong to this series.[16]

Schoenberner's book appears late in 1960 under the title *Der gelbe Stern* (The Yellow Star). It contains nearly two hundred photos documenting the persecution of the Jews in Europe.[17] Five of them come from the series that he discovered in Moscow.[18] As an epigraph to the introduction to the book, he cites a line of verse by Klabund: "Germany, you ought to forget neither the murdered, nor the murderers!"[19] The epigraph that he chose for translations of *Der gelbe Stern* is itself an epigraph: "Let others speak of their shame, I speak of mine"—written in 1933 by Bertold Brecht for his poem "*O Deutschland bleiche Mutter*" ("Oh Germany, pale mother").[20] Born two years before Hitler came to power, Gerhard Schoenberner had been strongly immunized against Nazism by his family environment since early childhood. His father and one grandfather were pastors. An uncle, Franz Schoenberner, was the last managing editor of the satirical magazine *Simplicissimus* before the *Gleichschaltung* began in March 1933.[21]

Because it is written without pathos, without posturing or outbursts, and in a "subdued tone,"[22] Gerhard Schoenberner's introduction to *Der gelbe Sterne* shows all the more powerfully what it must have been like for this young man in the late 1950s and early 1960s to have to confront both such a recent past and his compatriots, who did not want to see. He writes on the first page:

> What is shown in this book is our own deed. It happened through us, even if we did not commit it ourselves. We tolerated it—it concerns us. That is why we stand embarrassed before it and would prefer not to know about it. The persecution of the Jews was only one—but the most terrible—among countless others committed by the Nazis. It provides a particularly clear example of the inhuman nature of Nazi ideology and the criminal character of its practice. The mass murder of millions of innocent people was no perversion of National Socialism, but the logical application of its inherent principles. There is already an extensive literature on the phenomenon of antisemitism and on the gas chamber regime that was its dreadful realization. This book attempts to tell in pictures the story of the persecution of the Jews by the Third Reich. It is a book of the dead. All the people pictured here, unless exceptionally good fortune saved them, were murdered. Only their persecutors, unless exceptional misfortune took them, are still alive.[23]

Five of the eight photos reproduced here were made publicly available for the first time in that book of the dead, first published in Germany in 1960. They have not stopped circulating since.

Hanns Eisler, the composer for the music in *Night and Fog*, had been living in Berlin since 1925 but found himself in Vienna, where he had grown up and studied under Arnold Schoenberg, when Hitler came to power in January 1933. He was twenty-seven years old at the time. Jewish, a composer of committed works and numerous *Kampflieder* (battle songs), and a music critic for the Communist daily *Die rote Fahne* (The Red Flag)—although never a member of the Communist Party, Eisler is one of many artists, writers, and German politicians who were forced into exile to escape from a mother who had suddenly gone pale and was throwing into horror the "period of teeming intellectual development, social inventiveness, and cultural experimentation between the end of the Second Reich and the emergence of the Third."[24] Just one year before, Brecht had brought an entirely different *Mother* to the stage, based on the novel by Maxim Gorky and accompanied by the music of Hanns Eisler. A collaborative creation among many others, one which they worked on in Berlin before exile, then in California where they would find each other again in 1938, and again in Berlin—this time East Berlin—where Brecht and Eisler both ended up after being forced to leave the United States during the Cold War.

When distribution for the film is being organized in West Germany, Eisler recommends Brecht and his wife Helene Weigel as translators of the narration, which, he thought, would be of a "more concise and brutal" sort than the "too written" one of Jean Cayrol.[25] But in the middle of the Cold War, the Federal Republic of Germany is not going to risk having two East Berlin authors in charge of the work. During the same period, incidentally, the Federal Press Office (Bundespresseamt), which is responsible for covering the costs of the translation, simply attempts to have Eisler's name removed from the credits. But without success. At the suggestion of Cayrol himself, this translation of *Nuit et brouillard*, which was released in 1957 under the title *Nacht und Nebel*, was entrusted to the poet Paul Celan.[26] He who, in a speech he gave a little later when receiving the Bremen Literature Prize, said of the German language—his language:

> Reachable, near and not lost, there remained in the midst of the losses this one thing: language.
>
> It, the language, remained, not lost—yes, in spite of everything. But it had to pass through its own answerlessness, pass through frightful muting, pass through the thousand darknesses of death-bringing speech. It passed through and gave back no words for that which happened; yet it passed through this happening. Passed through and could come to light again, "enriched" by all this.[27]

Hanns Eisler composed the music for the anthem of the German Democratic Republic, which did not prevent him from defending the works of Schoenberg against denunciations by

Stalinist bureaucracy. In the Dorotheenstadt Cemetery in Berlin, where Brecht was buried in 1956 and Eisler in 1962, their tombstones face each other.[28]

The fact that Eisler's name appears even before Jean Cayrol's in the credits to *Nuit et brouillard* seems to indicate how important the musical score was to Resnais, who insisted that it be uninterrupted, "the only continuous voice in the entire film."[29] The sequence of the five photographs, including the one with the woman and the adolescents, arms crossed, is wordless but not silent. The brass and the flutes that accompanied the narrator's voice up to that point go silent just as he breaks off, and it is the stripped-down phrase of a violin that sustains the sequence of these photographs (it is as stripped-down as is the narrator's voice—that of actor Michel Bouquet, who later commented on "the difficult work of undercutting emotion" that Resnais had demanded of him, "of arriving every time at absolute neutrality in spite of the emotion [that he] felt").[30] Without necessarily being aware of it, the viewer thus finds him- or herself protected by this deep and calm melody from the potentially staggering effect of the wordless images. In some cases, later, nothing remains of this sequence but Eisler's phrasing, and then it is the photographs themselves that are being protected by the music, which brings them to mind without hammering at them, represents them without betraying them, with no more pathos or effect than Jean Cayrol's text and Michel Bouquet's voice in the film, or than Gerhard Schoenberner's introduction to his book of photographs, including those discovered in Moscow in a series from which the eight reproduced here are taken.

*

The Nazis used photography in a number of different ways, depending on the time, the place, and the circumstances. Even before they came to power, and right up to the war, photography was used as a particularly powerful tool for spreading the "pernicious epidemic"[31] of antisemitism promulgated by Minister of Propaganda Joseph Goebbels. In the form of cinematographic "newsreels," of radio programs. In the form of newspapers, particularly in the caricatures and articles appearing in that "news outlet for antisemitic hate," the weekly *Der Stürmer* (The Stormer), published by Julius Streicher, every issue of which—as well as its poster reproductions plastered all over Germany—bore the mantra of the Nazi religion in huge letters covering the bottom of the first page: "Die Juden sind unser Unglück!" (The Jews are our misfortune!).[32]

Victor Klemperer describes his constant run-ins with antisemitism before the war:

> I had a strange time with this unique (philologically speaking) language of the Third Reich.[33]
>
> Right at the outset, while I was still suffering no persecution, or at most a very mild form, I wanted to hear as little as possible of it. I had more than enough of it in the language of the window displays, the posters, the brown uniforms, the flags, the arms outstretched in the Hitler salute, the carefully trimmed Hitler moustaches. I took flight, I buried myself in my profession, I gave my lectures and desperately ignored the increasingly yawning gaps in the rows of seats in front of me, I exerted all my energies on my eighteenth-century French literature.[34] Why should I sour my life still further by reading Nazi publications when it was already being ruined by what was happening around me? If by chance or mistake a Nazi book fell into my hands I would cast it aside after the first paragraph. If the voice of the Führer or his Propaganda Minister was blaring out of a loudspeaker on the street I would give it a wide berth and when reading the newspaper I desperately tried to fish out the naked facts—forlorn enough in their nakedness—from the repulsive morass of speeches, commentaries and articles....
>
> I observed ever more closely how the workers in the factories spoke, how the beasts from the Gestapo spoke, and how we Jews expressed ourselves, caged in like animals in a zoo. There were no great differences to be registered; no, in fact there were absolutely none at all. Without a doubt, supporters and opponents, beneficiaries and victims, all conformed to the same models.
>
> I tried to get a grip on these models, a task that in some respects was extremely simple, since everything that was printed or spoken in Germany was standardized to conform to the official party line; anything that deviated in any way from the accepted pattern could not be made public. Books, newspapers, official communications and forms issued by administrative departments—all swam in the same brown sauce, and it was this absolute uniformity of the written language which explained the homogeneity of the spoken language.[35]

The photographers appointed by the regime provided the shots that would showcase the power of the Reich and the fervor of the crowds in the dailies and magazines. They also had to show Germans how the measures of exclusion were being carried out. This was the case on 1 April 1933 at the time of the boycott of Jewish-owned businesses. On that day, numerous display windows were marked with incitements: "Deutsche! Wehrt Euch! Kauft nicht bei Juden!" (Germans! Protect yourselves! Do not buy from Jews!), insults "Dreckjude" (shit-Jew), "Talmud-Gauner" (Talmud-crook), and huge stars outlined in paint.[36] This boycott, which was actually less successful than anticipated, was the subject of a long illustrated report in the *Völkischer Beobachter*, the organ of the National Socialist party, edited by Alfred Rosenberg, that had a circulation in excess of 300,000.[37] From the very beginning, and then according to the specific modalities of the subsequent phases of the antisemitic persecution, this one had its witnesses, at the same time as it had its victims and its perpetrators.[38] Photography brought all three of them together, regardless of whether they were present at the same time in the shot. For instance, the shot of the "shop-window language" during the boycott shows a notice stuck to the display window of a boutique that forced witnesses to see by ordering them to read so as to avoid the risk of being arrested: "Jewish business! Whoever shops here will be photographed!"[39] For the witnesses were not only those who, at the level of international states and institutions, looked or refused to look, helped or refused to help.[40] First of all, they were in Germany, in the "gulf [that] had opened up between the Jewish minority and the general population"—those witnesses who saw first-hand the abuses being perpetrated.[41] Those through whom the acts of persecution "happened, even if [they] did not do it [themselves],"[42] those who, tolerating it and looking away, or being indifferent to it, or going along with it "out of mental laziness, myopic calculation, stupidity, or pride," saw the violence of the Nazis being exercised even before they came to power and then in a legal framework starting in 1933.[43] Those who hated, tolerated, or agreed with the fanaticism of Hitler's own staccato rhetoric, "unspeakably inferior in kind, but magnetic in its effect on the masses: a weapon of definitely histrionic, even hysterical power, which he thrusts into the nation's wound and twists. He rouses the populace with images of his own injured grandeur, deafens it with promises, makes the people's sufferings into a vehicle for his own greatness."[44]

This fanaticism of the spoken word is on full display in the degradation shown in the propaganda, including the process whereby the propaganda itself creates that degradation. It exerts on the witnesses a totalitarian terror that targets "whatever someone is likely to do or think, so that any conduct, even exemplary conduct, never suffices to place one above suspicion."[45] Difficult, as a consequence, to know what to make of the often impassive look of adult witnesses in the photographs documenting the Nazi persecution of protesters and Jews. And the children, moving alongside the victims, ahead of them, marching, running, on bikes, laughing in the direction of the photographer in the way children laugh. But an onlooker can also go on his way. They are numerous, the witnesses, in the photographs of the Nazi terror during the period when it is being exercised throughout the German regions *vor aller Augen*, before everyone's eyes.[46] In small towns as well as large cities. In the streets and in the squares, perpetrators, victims, and bystanders fixed together on film. *Vor aller Augen*, the local offices of Communists and Social Democrats ransacked, their archives and flags burned, their militants arrested, beaten by the SS in front of crowds.[47] *Vor aller Augen*, men forced to wear signs around their necks stating the crime they committed: "Ich habe die Regierung beleidigt" (I insulted the government), "Ich habe den Schülern verboten, Heil Hitler zu sagen" (I forbade the schoolchildren to say "Heil Hitler"). *Vor aller Augen*, the woman with her head shaven—sometimes the work of a professional hairdresser, so the photograph's caption states—for having had sexual relations with a French prisoner of war or a Polish man subjected to forced labor. Shaven before being harnessed, like this one, with a placard that states in big letters that she, a *Polendirne* (whore for Poles) has sullied the honor of the German race.[48] Women who are then made to walk through the streets, in a kind of procession, in full view of young girls whose faces say nothing about what they are feeling and will later make of this scene, which they attended at their parents' sides.[49]

The Reich quickly drafted legal texts to expel the Jews from the German community, the so-called "Nuremberg Laws," the order to create them on the double having been given by Hitler on 13 September 1935 in the city of the same name during the annual meeting of the Party. On the double then, on 15 September 1935, one called "The Law for the Protection of German Blood and German Honor" and, then, to define its content more clearly, on 17 September, the "National Citizenship Law."

> It did not begin until 1935, when I was sitting over a newspaper in a Vienna coffeehouse and was studying the Nuremberg Laws, which had just been enacted across the border in Germany. I needed only to skim them and already I could perceive that they applied to me. Society, concretized in the National Socialist German state, which the world recognized absolutely as the legitimate representative of the German people, had just made me formally and beyond any question a Jew, or rather it had given a new dimension to what I had already known earlier, but which at the time was of no great consequence to me, namely that I was a Jew.
>
> What sort of new dimension? Not one that was immediately fathomable. After I read the Nuremberg Laws I was no more Jewish than a half hour before. My features had not become more Mediterranean-Semitic, my frame of reference had not suddenly been filled by magic power with Hebrew allusions, the Christmas tree had not wondrously transformed itself into the seven-armed candelabra. If the sentence that society has passed on me had a tangible meaning, it could only be that henceforth I was a quarry of Death. Well, sooner or later it claims all of us. But the Jew—and I now was one by decree of law and society—was more firmly promised to death, already in the midst of life. His days were a period of false grace that could be revoked at any second. . . .
>
> To be a Jew, that meant for me, from this moment on, to be a dead man on leave—someone to be murdered who only by chance was not yet where he properly belonged; and so it has remained, in many variations, in various degrees of intensity, until today. The death threat, which I felt for the first time with complete clarity while reading the Nuremberg Laws, included what is commonly referred to as the methodic "degradation" of the Jews by the Nazis. Formulated differently: the denial of human dignity sounded the death threat.[50]

In spite of this death threat, only a third of Germany's Jews would leave their country during the years following the Nazis' coming to power.

I remember conversations at home. My parents, my grandparents, my aunts and uncles, everyone was afraid because everyone knew that Hitler was an antisemite. But we had absolutely no idea, during those first two years, of what would befall us. Things changed drastically in 1935, with the promulgation of the racial laws. For me, as a pupil in elementary school, the worst shock was to be kicked out of school. One morning, the principal came and said "Niedermann, on your feet! You, you are Jewish, you cannot give the German salute. Take your things, you must leave and never come back." Such a terrible shock. I had just completed two years of elementary school. I had learned to read and write. And I was thrown out, then and there. Immediately.

From that moment on, we were not allowed to be seen in the tram anymore, we could no longer go to the pool, we could no longer go to the movies or the theatre, we could no longer enroll in German sports clubs. I no longer had contact with my friends in the neighbourhood. Even the young ones—they were all recruited for the Hitler Youth.

There were no ghettos in the relatively new German cities. Ghettos with walls did not exist. But, starting in 1935, we lived in a virtual ghetto. And that truly was the beginning of the end.[51]

Three years after these legal measures were put in place, a brief and violent episode of illegal persecution broke out during the so-called "Kristallnacht," the night of 9–10 November 1938. Incited by Goebbels, it was carried out by the SA, the "brown shirts" of the Nazi Party, who plundered and then set fire to apartments throughout the country and especially shops managed or owned by Jews. And synagogues. *Vor aller Augen*.[52] The one in Münster, in front of which pose the SA who set fire to it, laughing. The one in Ober-Ramstadt, at the foot of the Odenwald hills, which the municipal firefighters watch burn, saving their fire hose for the adjacent houses only.[53] At Edenkoben, a stopping-point on the German wine route, even if one catches only a glimpse of the silhouettes inside the bus, surrounded by onlookers, passing in front of the church, or hardly notices the suitcases on the roof, the writing on the sign hanging on the bus's front hood has a clarity about it that its author doubtless thought very funny: *Freifahrt nach Palästina* ("Free trip to Palestine").

In Mosbach, in the Baden region, a town of 5,079 inhabitants according to the 1933 census, three photographs of the central square taken at three separate distances—again, a church,

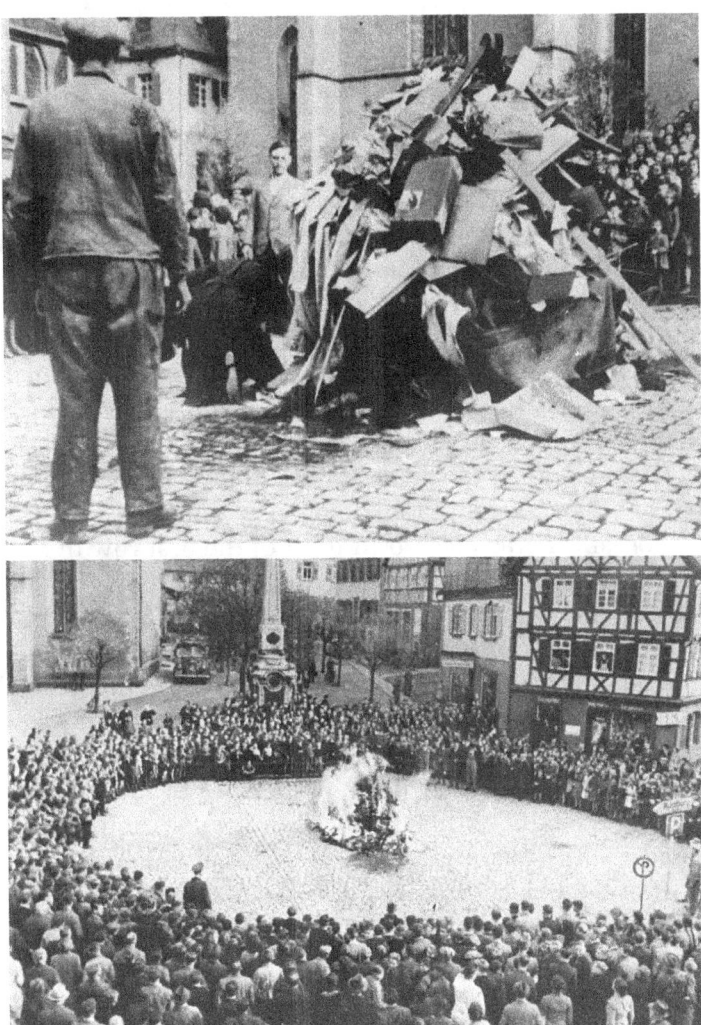

Figures 1 and 2. German civilians watch as the furnishings of the synagogue in Mosbach (Baden-Württemberg) are burned in the town's market square, 10 November 1938. USHMM, courtesy of the Hauptstaatsarchiv Stuttgart.

houses in half-timber with sloping roofs, pallid cobblestones, well-maintained—show objects piled up in a great heap in the middle of the square, objects taken from the synagogue that has been set on fire. Surrounding the heap, almost three hundred spectators. Not bystanders here, but people quite clearly invited specifically for the occasion, the number of whom is easy to judge given how neatly they are organized in compact and well-delineated rows. A real postcard of propaganda, then, the caption to which could well have been "How to prepare the population." Children and youth groups everywhere. They must have arrived from their classes, their workshops, their stores. The weather is clearly pleasant for 10 November, since most of them are not wearing coats. The spectacle has not yet started, and the photographer hired for the occasion, evidently situated on the second floor of one of the houses to get a view of the entire group, has probably caught the attention of the young people gathered there: a large number of them are turned toward the camera, heads raised, smiling joyfully. The wide angle of the shot allows us to see the flag bearing a swastika spread out above a store and, at the bottom of the shot, a row, also well-ordered, of very young children being taken into the square.

A good-sized area cleared in front of the first row of spectators is obviously meant to avoid one of them being suddenly hit by a spark. Waiting for the spectacle to start, they are there, watching. Some of them are talking to each other; we cannot hear what they are saying. This is doubtless from the same photographer who has come down from his elevated vantage point to take a close-up shot of the objects that have been brought out in front of the synagogue before they burn them. To better capture the details of this day on film, he goes into the space that had been left empty. The chairs are easily identifiable, but the rest of the objects are hard to make out; they are in pieces, placed in a heap for the impending bonfire. Perhaps they were smashed or torn off the walls of the synagogue. But they were probably sorted as they were being broken up on the square, as one does with branches for a fire, so that the pile is symmetrical and does not collapse prematurely. A pile that must indeed extend out the full two meters, judging by the men now standing in front of it—*now*, because neither of them is in the shot previously taken from above. The first, seen from the back in a laborer's work jacket, is wearing a hat. The second, from the front, is a young man, bareheaded, in a white shirt and vest. They clearly do not have the same function: the one in the work jacket being there to intervene if necessary; the one in white-collar there to direct and control the operation. Both of them are turned toward a third, he too in a work jacket, crouching at the foot of the pile, his right arm extended toward it. He may be about to light the fire, judging from the dark stains on the pristine ground, likely from the gasoline poured onto the pile. Only the cobblestones surrounding the pile are sullied. The men will have to clean up the stain a little later on, once the fire is extinguished and the ashes removed, while the spectators expressly brought there go back along the streets toward their classes, their workshops, their stores. In the meantime, they have become the witnesses. Will they speak of it in the coming days? What will they make of it later on, in their small town and in their heads? For now, the fire probably will take without difficulty. Thanks to the gasoline, or the drapes thrown onto the heap that reach the cobblestone at the spot where the man is crouched. Perhaps it is because of this fabric that he starts the fire at that spot. On his own initiative or following the instructions of the man in the vest. These drapes, which will in a moment go up in flames *vor aller Augen* on the Mosbach square this 10 November 1938, were probably the ones protecting the armoire where the scrolls of the Torah are kept in a synagogue.

These actions, initiated by Goebbels, were not appreciated by all the other higher-ups of the regime. Many worried that they could be harmful to Germany. First, in the face of world opinion, "what particularly strikes" the German ambassador in Washington, writing to Berlin on 14 November, "is the fact that, with few exceptions, the respectable patriotic circles, which are thoroughly anti-Communist and, for the greater part, antisemitic in their outlook, also begin to turn away from us." Second, in Germany, the violence in the streets had to be curbed since it could easily get out of hand and therefore become dangerous for the regime. And hugely expensive, as Göring would emphasize two days later: "If today a Jewish shop is destroyed, if merchandise is thrown into the street, the insurance company will pay the damages, and the Jew will have lost nothing." But the costs of removing the debris from the almost two hundred destroyed synagogues ended up being the responsibility of the Jewish communities themselves, by virtue of the legislation regarding real estate.[54]

> I have often been asked the question: Why did you not leave Germany, why did you not get out in time?[55] The basis of my response

has to do with my father. He had been a soldier in the German army for seven years, three before the First World War and then the four years of the war itself. He had suffered serious bodily injury because of shrapnel. He had lost an eye. He had been decorated with the Iron Cross first class, which is normally reserved for officers—which he was not. He was promoted to Sergeant at the end of seven years. How could he imagine that the people for whom he had given his blood and seven years of his life could do what they did to him? He could not believe it. He did not want to believe it. I remember vividly the slogan, posted all over the place in the country, of the Veterans Association of which he was a member: "You have earned the recognition of the homeland." When Kristallnacht took place, he was arrested and taken to Dachau for eight months.[56] Upon his return home, he had understood that indeed, they could very well do it. But by that time, it was too late.

Starting in 1935, we no longer had passports. And we no longer had any money either, because following Kristallnacht the Nazis levied a fine on Jewish communities. A fine for clearing the debris strewn across Germany following the destruction of Jewish property. That translated into the confiscation of all bank accounts and the collection of all valuable jewelry. So, I ask you, how is one to leave when one has no passport, no nationality—we no longer had German nationality—and no money? How is one supposed to emigrate?

Denounced, caricatured, harassed, stripped of their rights, expelled from the Reich through texts that produced "all imaginable forms of anti-Jewish harassment,"[57] the Jews of Germany would soon be expelled for good. On 22 October 1940, 6,540 of them are arrested,[58] most of them from the region of Baden, in particular from Mannheim and Karlsruhe, the others from Sarre and the Palatinate. They were given no advance notice; they were awoken at dawn; they were told to get their affairs in order; they were made to get into trucks; they were taken to the train station; their names were written on lists; they were made to wait for hours; they were crammed into train cars. Nine convoys in total. "Suicide attempts were relatively high; in almost all cases, they involved converts and assimilated Jews who had believed themselves to be insulated from the difficulties of the moment. With a brutal force, destiny threw them back into the very milieu that they had spent years, if not generations, trying with all their strength to leave. Psychologically, they were the least prepared to endure the sufferings of the Jews," explains the president of the Jewish community in Mannheim after the war.[59]

> At 4 o'clock in the morning, there was pounding on the door of the apartment where we lived.[60] Three Gestapo functionaries, in uniforms that we knew from the cinema, leather coats, soft hats. "Go, take what you can carry, you have the right to take 100 Reichsmarks, no more." They made us go down into the street. A small truck took us with other neighbors to the train station. The next day, all day, we were locked up in that station. 1,000 people. And, during the night of the next day, seven of the nine trains passed through the Karlsruhe station, and we were crammed into them. Everyone was terrified. People wondered whether we were being taken to Poland, like our Polish friends who had been deported. But, after twenty minutes, we can hear that we're crossing a bridge. You can hear it when you go over a bridge and, in any case, there was only one, large and made out of metal, and it crossed the Rhine in exactly twenty minutes. So people said: "But that's impossible, we are heading west. Where are we going?" We had already heard talk of the Madagascar solution and those things. . . .[61] We did not know where we were going. We had *no idea*. Nothing to eat or drink, and about the sanitation, well, I will say nothing. 6,500 people crammed into nine trains.

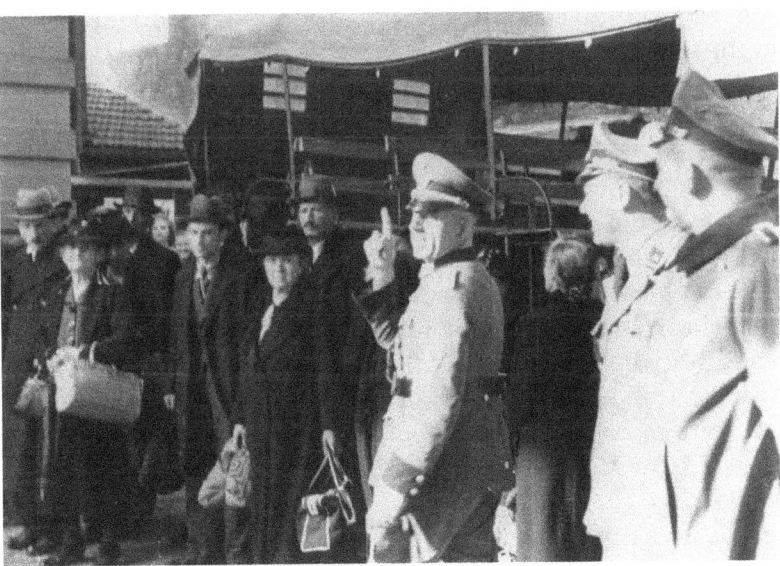

Figure 3. Jews from Lörrach and surroundings (Baden-Württemberg) are about to be herded onto trucks and then taken to deportation trains. 22 October 1940. USHMM, courtesy of the Stadtarchiv Lörrach (StaLö2.29.13).

Fifty-seven of the Jews arrested on this day, 22 October 1940, are from Mosbach, with its spotless cobblestones, and surrounding villages. Others are from Lörrach, a town close to the Black Forest and the Swiss border. The Kripo (Criminal Police) came to take them *vor aller Augen* at their homes and then lead them to the market square with their suitcases, packages, sometimes with knapsacks and heavy coats, then force them into the old business school, the façade of which one can see in the photographs, and register them and then make them leave again. The shots were taken by the assistant to the Chief of the Criminal Police, explains the caption.[62] A police officer, forefinger raised, slightly turned toward two colleagues behind him, must be making some joke because the two of them are smiling, looking at him. What kind of joke? We do not know what those among these men and women—most of them elderly—who heard the joke because they were standing near the police officer in front of the school must have felt. Those already registered or about to be. What word-of-mouth could have brought the onlookers here, pressed in behind the two policemen who keep them separated from the arrestees? Or, those who watch from their windows and are clearly of the same generation as those who are leaving—what do they think of this departure?

Then the Jews of Lörrach are herded onto open trucks covered with tarps. Rows of benches have been installed for the operation. We do not know how many of them will still be alive in 1942 when the transport will go in the opposite direction, from the south of France toward Auschwitz.[63] If the coats worn by these women and men, especially the older ones, tell of their uncertainty about where they will be taken, judging by the relatively light clothing worn by the onlookers, both young and old, who are watching the covered trucks full of people who were still their neighbors just the day before, the temperature in Lörrach must have been mild on 22 October 1940, as it was in Mosbach two years earlier when other onlookers came to watch the chairs and the drapes of the synagogue being burned in the square.[64] No doubt, Julius Streicher, editor of *Der Stürmer*, was only too pleased to see the departure of the covered trucks, just as he was probably not unhappy with the symmetry of the remark he made one day in 1936 when, passing through Lörrach, he wrote in the city's guest book: "Ohne die Lösung der Judenfrage, keine Endlösung des deutschen Volkes" (literally: without the solution to the Jewish Question, no final solution for the German people).[65]

The nine convoys of Jews from Germany who were no longer German would indeed depart westward. Their destination was the station at Oloron-Sainte-Marie in the Low-Pyrenees. The village of Gurs lies eighteen kilometers to the west of the station. There, on alluvial terrain that heavy rains frequently turn into a quagmire, more than four hundred wooden barracks were built in forty days in the spring of 1939 to house the almost 20,000 refugees arriving from Spain at the time of the fall of the Republic, others having been divided up among various "housing centers" opened in the Southern areas, at Argelès, Saint-Cyprien, Agde, Rivesaltes, Le Vernet . . .

> The next morning, the trains stopped at a small station.[66] I know today that it was Oloron-Sainte-Marie, beside Pau. And, of course, it was raining. It always rains there. Or almost always. And we eventually figured out that it was the Pyrenees, probably because there were people among us who had been there before. And they said: "It's the south of France." They made us get into covered trucks, trucks that had a military look, of the police or the mobile guards, or what remained of the French army.

The first of these German Jews, torn away from their existence just two days earlier, enter the Gurs camp on Thursday, 24 October 1940. In the history books, this is the date of the meeting between Pétain and Hitler at the train station in Montoire-sur-le-Loir. Filmed and photographed by the Germans, their handshake "was seen the world over and triggered a flurry of questions."[67] The military cap worn by the Führer makes it difficult to tell if the soldier in the background is taking a photograph or if he's making a film of the scene.[68] The following Thursday, Marshall Pétain broadcasts a speech on the radio to explain the significance of the meeting to the French people: "A collaboration has been envisioned between our two countries. I accepted this in principle. The forms this will take will be discussed later." The internment of German Jews in Gurs on the same day clearly indicates that, contrary to the Marshall's claim, not all of these "forms" had to wait to be discussed. But it is true that the arrival of the first of the nine convoys at the station in Chalon-sur-Saône triggered lively discussions: It had a difficult time getting permission to cross the French Demarcation Line. To get rid of the Jews, the German government had claimed they were from Alsace-Lorraine. The French government, furious at not having been informed, protested vehemently before the German Armistice Commission in Wiesbaden, to which it indicated that it refused to see the Unoccupied Zone become "a spillway for persons deemed undesirable on the territory of the Reich."[69] But it was defeated; it finally gave in and, on French orders, 6,500 Jewish men, women, and children from the regions of Baden, Sarre, and Palatinate, undesirables everywhere, were taken to the Gurs camp. When it first opened, the site had been called "Hosting Center for Spanish Refugees." A memo sent on 21 October 1940 by the Vichy Minister of the Interior to clarify what kind of discipline to use in the camps informed the Prefect of the Low-Pyrenees that Gurs would be a "semi-repressive camp."[70]

That this memo coincides with the arrest of the German Jews on the very next day might simply be fortuitous; indeed, the various disagreements regarding the nine convoys suggest as much. Nonetheless, it is very much the case that they were both in keeping with the times. On 25 October, a note from the Minister of Foreign Affairs remarks that "it is at the very least inopportune, at the moment when we are struggling to rid France of the greatest possible number of foreigners, especially when it involves Israelites, to welcome thousands of German Jews onto our territory."[71] In order to avoid French protests, the German "spillway" operations in the southern zone became more discrete, and "Vichy officials seem to have been as eager to keep Jewish refugees out of the Unoccupied Zone as German officials were to keep them from returning to the Occupied Zone." As a 1941 compendium of new regulations concerning Jews puts it concisely: "The Demarcation Line is closed in both directions to Jews."[72]

*

On the 18th of this same month of October, 1940, the "law pertaining to foreign nationals of Jewish race" was printed in the

Journal officiel. The first article stipulates that "aliens of the Jewish race can be interned in special camps, from the date of the enactment of this law, through a decision of the prefect in the department of their residence." Signed by Marshall Pétain and three of his ministers on 4 October, this law is reproduced on page 5,324 of the 18 October 1940 issue of the *Journal officiel*. On the preceding page, the law from the day before (3 October 1940), signed by Marshall Philip Pétain and nine of his ministers, is the "law on the status of the Jews." We know that those in charge of Vichy, "complicit even before having understood the inevitable extent of their own compromise," did not wait for it to be imposed by the occupying power before enacting it.[73] We also know that whereas the German ordinance of the preceding month defined Jews by "religion," the French statute of 3 October defined them by "race."[74]

On the very day that the "law on the status of the Jews" appeared in the *Journal officiel*, the Chief of Staff of the Ministry of Foreign Affairs sent a long telegram to the French ambassador in Washington outlining the reasons for this law:[75]

> Anticipating trends in public opinion that will arise in the United States as a consequence of the publication of the law regarding the status of Jews, I shall point out in what follows the arguments your services could use to explain the reasons that have motivated the decisions of the government.
>
> Before the war, France had a reduced number of Israelites and antisemitism was, so to speak, unknown in the years following the war. The Israelites came to France in ever growing numbers beginning in 1936, profiting from the commanding influence of the Israelite element in the Popular Front. They entered in the hundreds of thousands, overcoming barriers that a powerless administration tried in vain to erect and speaking as masters when they encountered any difficulties, as our agents who found themselves in contact with them can attest. The reaction was as inevitable in France as it has been in countries where the Jews have exercised power at any given moment.
>
> Among the French Jews themselves, aside from some excellent individuals who are both trustworthy and loyal, it is only too true that their very specific mentality has caused a great number of them to attack all the ideas from which, despite an eventful national history, the French had never distanced themselves. The Israelites who have held positions of power between 1936 and 1940 have particularly distinguished themselves in this regard:

One has only to recall the language used by M. Jean Zay about the French flag[76] and about the book published by M. Léon Blum on marriage.[77]

We have thus been led to the conviction that one of the conditions for national recovery was the removal of Israelites from a certain number of careers that allow them to exercise a harmful influence on our administrations, on public opinion, and on our youth. No spirit of reprisal has inspired the law that has just been promulgated. To the contrary, it could prevent outbreaks of antisemitic movements, the excesses of which would be difficult to contain. Furthermore, it is important to point out that no measures were taken against persons or property. The new arrangements aim to resolve, definitively and dispassionately, a problem that had become particularly serious, and to allow the peaceable existence in France of individuals whose racial character makes them dangerous when they get too closely involved in our political and administrative life.

Other laws had been passed two years earlier, during peacetime, but xenophobia had never stopped mounting, especially since a large number of refugees had arrived from Germany starting in 1933. Xenophobia was fomented by an extreme right that had distorted to its climax the already old alteration of the word *métèque*. No longer foreigners with rights of citizenship in an ancient Greek city, but intruders or parasites to be urgently hunted down.[78] It is in this context that Édouard Daladier, although president of the radical party, becomes the head of a right-wing government on 10 April 1938. Breaking with the Republican tradition, this government uses decree-laws to worsen the situation of foreigners of every kind, immigrants or refugees, through a "headlong rush into nationalist-security politics."[79] The tone is established immediately. A memo dated 14 April from the Minister of the Interior to the prefects explains why it is necessary to "rid our country of the undesirable foreign elements who circulate and who act with no regard for the laws or regulations."[80] Even better than the articles themselves of the decree-laws dated 2 May and 12 November 1938, obscured as these are by legal terminology, are the "reports" preceding them that clearly show what the rhythm of this "headlong rush" was. The use of the word "hospitality," which was central for the Republican tradition of that time, was reversed within a period of six months, even though the text from 2 May was intended to protect refugees.

These reports are formally addressed to the President of the Republic, Albert Lebrun. Daladier to Lebrun, 2 May 1938:

> Mr. President, etc. It should be noted from the outset—and to highlight the character of the text, which is subject to your high endorsement—that the present draft decree-law has in no way modified the regular conditions of access to our soil, and that it does not breach the traditional rules of French hospitality, of the spirit of liberalism and of humanity that is one of the most noble features of our national spirit.

Again Daladier to Lebrun, 12 November 1938: "Mr. President, etc. The decrees of the 2nd and the 14th of last May,[81] which regulate the situation of foreigners in France, clearly emphasize the distinction that the government was seeking to make between morally doubtful individuals who are not worthy of our hospitality, and the healthy and hardworking portion of the foreign population."[82] The words used in this report from 12 November 1938 are pointed, even if we avoid interpreting them anachronistically by lending them a weight they did not have then. It is "indispensable to ensure the rigorous elimination of undesirables." But not everyone can be expelled, particularly those for whom "it is impossible to find a country that will accept them." In that case, it is important to

> assign them a residence in a determined locality, but for those foreigners who, due to their legal history or any activity that poses a danger to national security, cannot, without peril to the public order, enjoy this still too-grand liberty, it is necessary to keep them under house arrest. It also seemed indispensable to direct this category of foreigners toward special centers where they would be subject to permanent surveillance, justified by their repeated infractions of the rules of hospitality.... Please accept, Mr. President, etc.

"Title IV" of this decree from 12 November 1938 announces "measures relative to certain undesirable aliens." Hospitality is no longer what it once was, and the expression "undesirable aliens" is on the verge of becoming redundant.

From one day to the next in September 1939, because the country has just declared war on Germany, all German Jews, along with other opponents of Nazism and Austrians who had taken refuge in France over the course of the preceding years or months, become "undesirable aliens" in the absurd and appalling application of the 1938 decrees. War is declared on 3 September 1939 and, on 5 September, a communiqué reproduced in the newspapers and on the radio calls on "alien nationals of territories belonging to the enemy," in this case men between the ages of seventeen and fifty, to report to one of the fifty camps opened specifically for them. The characterization of the Jews as aliens will soon be key to the success of the collaborationist press, in particular *Je suis partout*, where one author writes in 1941 that "the Jewish problem must be solved because the Jew is an alien, because he is the enemy, because he pushed us into war, and because it is right that he should pay."[83]

> After serious opposition, after having trained, bargained, discussed, shed some false tears, the adherents of Vichy, victims of their own game, would resolutely agree to violate the sacred right of asylum, to give over herds of men and women, children, and rosy-cheeked babies to the detested enemy who had marked them for certain death.
> Of course, it was only a matter of "aliens," of "the stateless," not of the French! The spared life of the French had been purchased at the cost of those of the aliens; one was very proud of it.
> Later, the life of the non-Jewish French will be purchased for the price of the life of the Jewish French; one will be very proud of it.
> Up until there was no longer a market to close. Then it became clear that we were all "sold out."
> And the lesson will serve no one.[84]

Refugee. National. Turned away. Alien. Jew. In France. "It is right that he should pay." A brief history of an alien Jewish family by means of the only archives of the French administration. Leopold Feiertag was born in Munich in 1901. His wife Anna, in Vienna in 1905, like their two children, Kurt in 1926 and Elisabeth in 1928. They sought refuge in France in November 1938. In Rouen, where the father is a laborer, the son a fitter. At the beginning of the war, they are in Loiret but are then expelled, toward Nièvre, because they are German.

30 September 1939, telegram regional commander of the general staff to the Nevers subdivision: "Receive tomorrow nineteen non-suspect German nationals with five children expelled from Loiret and subject only to the general measures concerning aliens. Make agreement with Prefect arrange for them housing and possible employment in agricultural work."

16 November 1939, general staff 5th region, Orleans, to Nevers special commissary: Request for information on German women nationals expelled from Loiret currently housed in Nevers.

23 November 1939, Nevers special commissary to general staff 5th region, Orleans: "I have the honor of sending to you the information that you have requested, etc." Among these German women nationals, Anna Feiertag. "Married, mother of 2 children: Kurt 13 years and Babette 11 years. Previously lived 21 rue du Pavé in Rouen (Seine Inférieure). . . . Currently residing at the Maison du Peuple in Nevers. Wants to stay in this latter city. No means of subsistence."

30 October 1940, Nevers, Prefecture of the Nièvre, Cabinet of Prefect, letter to "child Feiertag Curt [sic], 17 rue de Chauvelles Nevers": It is a form to be filled out. The ellipses are of course not in the original.

> I have the honor of acquainting you with the terms of instruction that have been addressed to me . . . declaration on October 20 which is binding upon every Jew . . . a matter of urgency that you return this completed form to me . . . identity cards of Jewish persons must have a special stamp . . . present yourself to the Prefecture of Nièvre (Identity Card Services) before November 5 to get the special stamp. . . . If you do not have an identity card . . . before November 5 . . . two identity photographs . . . tax stamp of 13 francs so that the card can be immediately delivered to you. . . . Highest consideration. On behalf of the Prefect, the Secretary General.

Father or mother corrected the spelling of "Kurt" when they filled out the form. "Profession: None." "Religion: Jewish." "Length of uninterrupted stay in France: November 1, 1938."

4 July 1942, Nevers, 17 rue de Chauvelles: Arrest of Leopold, Anna, and Kurt Feiertag. Driven back the same day to Loiret, from which they had been expelled on 1 October 1939, to be interned at the Pithiviers camp.

15 July 1942, Regional Prefect to the Prefect of Loiret: Ellipses, once again.

> The chief of German Security Police has asked me to confirm with you the decision . . . the healthy Jews currently at the Pithiviers camps . . . will be transferred on July 17, departure: 6:15. Boarding will take place on July 16 from 19:00 to 21:00 in the presence of German authorities . . . every Jew must bring 3 days' worth of food supplies . . . the Jews transferred must have a yellow star visible on all clothing, and in addition must have their heads shaved. They will not be allowed to keep a coat, a razor, a watch, jewelry, or money. They will be allowed to keep only their wedding band. The controls must be completed on Thursday before 19:00, so that the boarding can take place at exactly the specified time.
>
> I would be much obliged if you would give the necessary instructions for the preparation of this departure and in particular provide the order to accompany the convoy to the station at Pithiviers. A detachment of police will provide 10 police officers in rotation to guard the train continuously during the night, concurrently with German police officers. . . . Prepare the list of Jews transferred to the camp at Pithiviers in four copies to be remitted to the chief of the detachment . . . at your earliest convenience, copy in duplicate of this list. . . . On behalf of the Regional Prefect: The Deputy Police Superintendent. Copy to the Regional Prefect.

16 July 1942, stamp of Nièvre Prefecture on the regional prefect letter, Dijon, to the prefect of Nièvre, Nevers, 13 July 1942:

> Following my cable of July 11 and in conformity with instructions from the German authorities, I have the honor of informing you that, following the arrests, the Jewish children who remain behind after the departure of their parents, as well as handicapped or other Jews requiring care or other kinds of assistance, cannot be assisted by the French Red Cross or by French welfare associations or other French services. Only the imposed Jewish association Union Générale des Israélites de France is permitted to ensure this care, with no exceptions. On behalf of the Regional Prefect, the Director of the Cabinet.

Remark in pencil at the bottom of the letter: "to be sent by c.c. [*copie conforme*, certified copy] for all purposes to the Chief of the Second Division, the Inspector of Support Services, the Health Inspector, Nevers, July 17, 1942. The Prefect."

16 July 1942, Nevers Police Commissioner to the Prefect of Nièvre 1st Division, 2nd Bureau, Aliens: "List of children whose Jewish parents have been arrested over the course of the month of July." On this list, "Feiertag Babette, thirteen years old, current address: 6 bis rue du Donjon, Nevers." On some unknown date, Babette has been taken to the Drancy camp, since one finds the following in the archives of the UGIF's homes for children: *9 November 1942*, transferred from Drancy to the UGIF children's home on rue Lamarck, in Paris. *24 November 1942*, the director of the Larmarck Centre informs the mayor of the 19th Arrondissement that Elisabeth Feiertag had been taken to the Claude Bernard hospital. Stayed in a children's home until 4 November 1943. After that, no one knows.

17 July 1942, 6:15 a.m.: Departure of Transport 6 from the Pithiviers station toward Auschwitz. 928 Jews deported. Some are French, including 20 born in France. The majority are aliens. 809 men and 119 women. Among them are 24 youth, between twelve and seventeen years old.

19 July 1942: arrival of Transport 6 at Auschwitz.

1945: About 80 survivors from Transport 6. Leopold, Anna, and Kurt Feiertag are not among them.

There is one more document to add to this brief history of an alien Jewish family found in the French administrative archives. Like almost all the documents already cited, it too is housed in the Regional Archives of Nièvre. A letter written in blue ink. It has the registration stamp of the Prefecture on it. Its careful use of French lets pass a certain turn of phrase—"to see what is that which"—where one can almost hear their voices, their intonations. A letter signed by forty people. Among them, Anna Feiertag.

Nevers, 14 December 1940
Mr. Prefect,
We simply cannot leave the community center without expressing to you, Mr. Prefect, our profound gratitude for all that you have done for us in Nevers.

> As refugees from Germany and Austria, we have already had occasion to experience the generosity of France, a country of asylum for all persecuted people.
>
> And it is in one of the most difficult moments for us that we have had the chance once again to see what is that which is the good heart and the dedication of the French people.
>
> We assure you, Mr. Prefect, that we will never forget this generosity, and that we will always remember what France did for us with profound gratefulness.
>
> Please accept, Mr. Prefect, our most sincere feelings.[85]

*

No longer *vor aller Augen*, the onlookers are less frequent when German Jews start being deported from Germany toward the east—for real this time—in 1941 and 1942. But it is still dark night on that 10 December 1941, according to the photograph's caption, when about twenty people are sent into the yard of a château in a small town in the Rhineland, wearing that yellow star on their coats, mandated three months earlier.

> Today I ask myself again the same question I have asked myself and all kinds of people hundreds of times; which was the worst day for the Jews during those twelve years of hell?
>
> I always, without exception, received the same answer from myself and others: 19 September 1941. From that day on it was compulsory to wear the Jewish star, the six-pointed Star of David, the yellow piece of cloth which today still stands for plague and quarantine, and which in the Middle Ages was the color used to identify the Jews, the color of envy and gall that has entered the bloodstream; the yellow piece of cloth with "Jew" printed on it in black, the word framed by the lines of two telescoped triangles, the word consisting of thick block capitals, which are separated and given broad, exaggerated horizontal lines to effect the appearance of the Hebrew script.[86]
>
> The description is too long? But no, on the contrary! I simply lack the ability to pen precise, vivid descriptions. Many was the time when it came to sewing a new star onto a new piece of clothing (or rather an old one from the Jewish clothing store), a jacket or a work coat, many was the time that I would examine the cloth in minute detail, the individual specks of the yellow fabric, the irregularities of the black imprint—and all of these individual segments would not have been sufficient, had I wanted to pin an agonizing experience with the star on each and every one of them.[87]

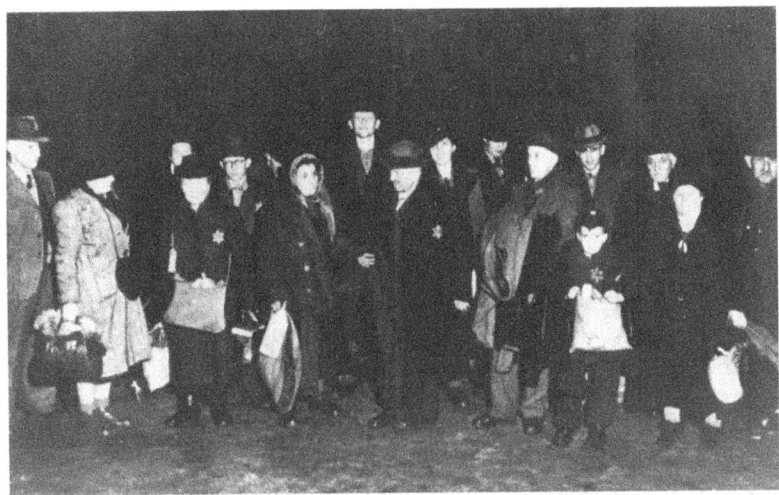

Figure 4. German Jews from Coesfeld (North Rhine-Westphalia) are rounded up for deportation to Riga, Latvia, 10 December 1941. USHMM, courtesy of Fred Hertz.

The caption in *Vor aller Augen* states that the shot was taken at dawn, on the orders of the Gestapo, by one of the town's professional photographers. The high quality of the framing, the focus, and the lighting make sense, then: the photographer must have used a standing lamp to get such professional lighting, fixed at exactly the right height, that brings out the details of the faces, the coats worn or folded over arms, and, around the neck of the only child in the group, the grain of the fabric on a bag and the metallic shine of a flask coming out of this bag. The flask and the extra coats are not superfluous. These people are going to be sent by truck to Münster, where the members of the SA were laughing in 1938 in front of the burning synagogue. Three days later, the convoy will leave, deporting them to the north in this month of December, to the Riga ghetto, in Latvia.[88]

The photographer must have had the standing lamp in his studio, as he had been practicing his trade in this small town since the beginning of the thirties. Or so it is explained on the city hall's website on the occasion of an exhibition the municipality organized a half-century later in honor of the local artist. The artist who had captured so many cherished family memories: communions, birthdays, marriages, and other "precious life moments," says the site. The artist who had photographed celebrations, work scenes, activities of artisans, and "the typical character" of the surrounding countryside better than anyone else. The destructions, too, endured by the city during the war, and the reconstruction just after. This photographer, did he keep in his studio the shots he took in the yard of the château at daybreak on 10 December 1941? Thirty years after his death, did the organizers of the exhibition dedicated to him think to show the deportation of twenty of their fellow citizens as part of the destruction that their small town had suffered during the war?

But *vor aller Augen* again, in the Main valley, when, once the Jews have been taken away, what used to be their clothing and their furniture is auctioned off in front of what used to be their house, to neighbors who stumble upon all kinds of treasures. And *vor aller Augen* a final time, in the Jewish cemetery in the North Rhine-Westphalian city of Altena where burials used to take place (when Jews still had the right to be there), three photos, taken in 1943. A man in coveralls, under the watchful and serious gaze of his colleagues—all quite elderly, since the young are at the front—in the city's emergency technical service, uses a welding torch to unsolder the finely-crafted iron gate surrounding one of the tombstones. Another took care of the gate to the cemetery, beginning with the Star of David affixed to the top. It is 1943; the country needs iron. These members of the emergency technical service of Altena wear safety glasses to protect their eyes from getting burned by what they are doing.

*

In conjunction with the Ministry of Propaganda, in 1937 the Wehrmacht establishes the Propaganda Kompanien (PK), consisting of journalists, photographers, and cameramen. Their name leaves no doubt about their role. From the beginning of the war, the photos and films produced by these PK in the Occupied Territories—as the same shots were being taken by the many amateur photographers among the soldiers—were immediately sent to Berlin in order to feed newspapers columns and the cinematographic newsreels where propaganda was to take the place of information.[89]

Poland is invaded on 1 September 1939 and on 2 October, the on-site command of the PK receives an order from the Minister of Propaganda that at least has the merit of clarity: "What we want are images of Jews at work. This material is intended to reinforce our antisemitic propaganda here and abroad."⁹⁰ What is more, the PK had carte blanche to send to Berlin whatever seemed interesting to them. Like this photograph, of soldiers taking pictures.

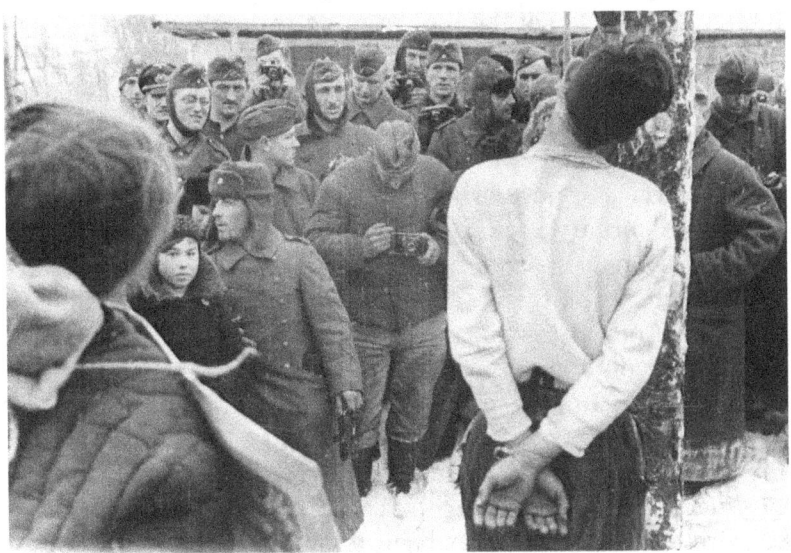

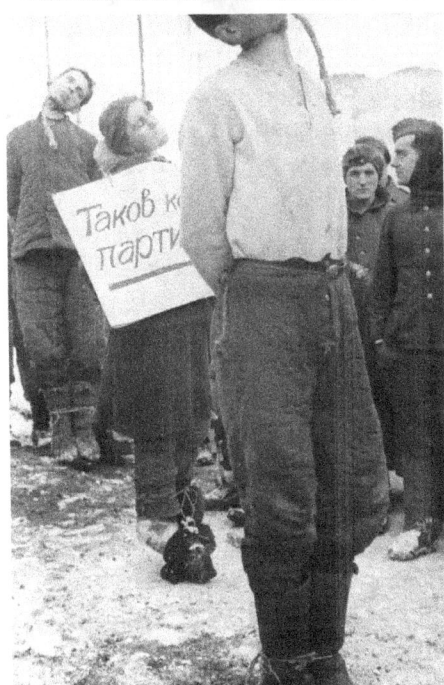

Figures 5 and 6. 1941 or 1942, near Orel (220 miles south of Moscow). German soldiers, members of a Propaganda Kompanie, take photographs of three Russian partisans who have been hanged. The placard around the woman's neck reads (in Russian): "This is how partisans end." USHMM, courtesy of the Bundesarchiv (Bild 101I/287/0872/28 and 101I/287/0872/28A).

Will these men keep as "trophies" in their wallets these shots that they took on that day, their feet in the snow of a Russian winter?[91] Those at the back probably will not have captured the writing on the sign around the neck of the hanged person in their shot, unlike the soldier in the first row who seems to be taking his time to get the best framing. And how have the two young girls ended up at such a spectacle? Who brought them there? One of them seems to be trying to shield her vision, whereas you can think that the face of the hanged person will remain in the memory of the other child, who is looking at her.

The service report of one Propaganda Kompanie for the month of February 1941 gives an example of what the fieldwork of these teams consisted of (here, that of PK 689 in the Lodz ghetto in Poland), thanks to which Germans would be able to see images of those who actually were the Jews of the East: on the 12th, a photographer takes seven shots in the ghetto; on the 12th and 13th, two cameramen make a film there; from the 17th to the 19th, a journalist files a report from there. As for the photographs taken in the Warsaw ghetto in June 1941, the *Berliner Illustrierte Zeitung* uses them for a photographic dossier presented to its readers beginning in the following month, which comes at an opportune moment since the invasion by German troops of the territory of the Soviet Union had begun on 22 June. This dossier, entitled "The Jews among Themselves," shows "how those who spawned the criminals from Bromberg, Lemberg, Dubno, and Bialystok live. Reportage in the Warsaw ghetto."[92]

Photography has been very popular in Germany since the 1920s, most notably thanks to Leica, the pioneer of film cameras in 24 x 36 mm, Minox, and Zeiss Icon (in 24 x 24)—formats that make the cameras particularly easy to transport. Soldiers often carry them in their military bags.[93] So, while they are contributing to the collections the Propaganda Kompanien send to Berlin, they can also keep some for themselves, to send to their spouses or fiancées—images that for some, perhaps, are bound to enhance the family album, alongside the memories of birthdays and marriages and other "precious life moments."

For SS-man Kurt Franz, life's precious moments—the good times—include the years when he was taking part in programs of the extermination of the mentally ill, then in the extermination of Jews in Bełżec and Treblinka, camps for which he served as the last commandant in the fall of 1943. At least, if the title that he gave his photo album of those years, found by the police at the time of his arrest in 1959, is to be believed: *Schöne Zeiten*.[94] An amateur photographer, Kurt Franz also knew how to wield the pen. In fact, he even wrote lyrics—he probably found this hilarious—for a song that the camp's surviving deportees were forced to sing: "For us, there is no today other than Treblinka, our destiny. . . . We wish to serve, and serve again, until good fortune, one day, smiles on us. Hurrah!"[95]

*

On 1 September 1939, when the Wehrmacht invades Poland, it is flanked by units known by the name of Einsatzgruppen der Sicherheitspolizei, task forces of the security police. Comprising more than three thousand men from various police corps, these groups were formed by Heydrich, chief of the Reichssicherheitshauptamt (RSHA) beginning in the fall of 1939. Heydrich is the deputy of the one whom the orders, reports, and other correspondence at all the levels of Nazi administration, without needing to name him, always call by the title of Reichsführer-SS, in other words Himmler, himself Hitler's "direct substitute."[96] These men of the Einsatzgruppen, whose leaders "belong in the fish pond of Nazi intellectuals recruited by Heydrich," have as their principal task "the systematic arrest of all potential enemies."[97] There is no shortage of names for these enemies in Nazi rhetoric: Jews, Communists, Judeo-Bolsheviks, Bolshevik operators, communist intelligentsia, Judeo-Bolshevik intelligentsia. . . . On 22 June 1941, when the Wehrmacht invades the USSR, on the first day of "Operation Barbarossa,"[98] it is accompanied by similar units, soon also called Einsatzgruppen, this time composed mainly of members of the Order Police and the Waffen-SS, the military branch of the SS.[99] The invaded territory is divided into four areas from the north to the south, from the Baltic to the Black Sea, in which four Einsatzgruppen will work—A, B, C, D—each comprised of different commandos, the Einsatz- and the Sonderkommandos.[100]

The myth of a Wehrmacht free of all responsibility for the atrocities committed in the East—for which the SS alone would be found guilty—was going to last in the postwar period.[101] Indeed, goaded by the anticommunism and antisemitism of its leaders, the army had participated extensively in acts of violence committed in the field. To carry out their mission as efficiently as possible, the Einsatzgruppen could not allow their actions to be hindered by international military conventions governing the protection of civilians—conventions that, in principle, applied to the Germany army. This question was examined during the months of secret preparation for Operation Barbarossa, and on 26 April 1941, the High Command of the Wehrmacht explicitly authorized the Sonderkommandos to "[carry out] the executive measures regarding the civilian population in the context of their mission and on their own responsibility."[102] With the goal of efficiency in mind and given the high number of Jews in the USSR, these commandos were not working alone. Depending on the time period and location, but also on the conditions and specific motivations, local auxiliaries were recruited without difficulty.[103] The results obtained were commensurate with the assigned mission: between summer 1941 and spring 1943, from the Baltic to the Black Sea, more than a million Jews were exterminated.

From that moment onward, the time had passed for using photography to instruct Germans about specimens of Polish Jews. These were still living Jews. In the East, beginning in the summer of 1941, the time had come for death, and those in charge took stock of the risk they would run in sending images of the extermination back to Germany. The risk of seeing those who until then had been indifferent, pleased, or even enthusiastic be moved to feel pity, become outraged, or even start thinking about the Jews as human beings in their own right. It was no longer a question of showing, therefore, but rather of concealing. It was now prohibited to photograph "executions," as they were called in all official documents, whether of Jews or all other enemies, military or civilian, that the Reich must suppress in its battle. But the fact that both the SS and the Wehrmacht had to issue this written interdiction on repeated occasions throughout the duration of the war shows the limits of its efficacy, illustrated in a particularly sinister way once again in 1943 by a shot that shows ten hanged men with a sign fixed to the central post of the gallows bearing the underlined notice: "Fotografieren verboten!" (Photography prohibited!).[104]

These words make for clear reading. The orders restating this prohibition constitute a kind of photography in words of the acts for which there were to be no images. In matters of obedience, regulation, and prohibition, it was only right that the Waffen-SS should lead by example. "It is prohibited," its regulatory bulletin states from 11 June 1941, "to take photographs of executions within or outside of the territory of the German Reich. It is also prohibited to encourage people not belonging to the Waffen-SS to take photographs of the executions. The authorization to take shots for reasons of service can only be given by the heads of the command posts of the police. Any shots produced on this day must be confiscated and destroyed."[105] On 12 and 13 July 1941, more than 3,000 Jewish men are killed by members of two battalions of the Ordnungspolizei near the Polish city of Białystok. In the confidential order that he sent to the commanders of these battalions regarding this intention on the day before, the colonel of the police regiment clarified: "The executions will take place away from cities, villages, and public roads. The pits will be leveled off in such a way as to prevent them from becoming sites of pilgrimage. I forbid the taking of photographs and the presence of spectators on the grounds of the executions." The follow-up to this order highlights the colonel's concern about what "impressions" the police officers might have at the end of such an *Aktion*: "The battalion and company commanders are required especially to provide for the spiritual needs of the men who participate in this action. The impressions of the day are to be blotted out through evening social events. Furthermore, the men are to be continuously reminded of the political necessity of the measures."[106]

General Wöhler is the military Chief of Staff of the 11th Army, the regiment that actively facilitates the crimes of the Einsatzgruppe D directed by Otto Ohlendorf. Which does not stop him—even after the soldiers of his army participate in the massacres of Jews perpetrated in Bālti (in today's Moldova) by the Romanian troops of the German-allied Conducātor (Leader) Antonescu[107]—from sending out an order on 22 July 1941 in which he plays at defending the German sense of honor and "normal sensitivity" in the face of the oriental conception of human life.

> In view of a special circumstance," he writes, "the following has to be pointed out explicitly. Given the conception of human life that predominates in eastern Europe, German soldiers may become witnesses to events (mass executions, the killing of civilian prisoners, Jews, and others) which they cannot prevent at this time but which violate German feelings of honor most deeply. For every normal person it goes without saying that one does not take photographs of such disgusting excesses or report about them when writing home. The making or spreading of photographs or reports about such events will be regarded as a subversion of decency and discipline in the army and will be punished severely. All pictures, negatives, and reports of such excesses are to be collected and sent to the Ic/AO of the army. To contemplate such events with curiosity . . . is beneath the dignity of a German soldier.[108]

At the same time, the nature and the intensity of the massacres were enough to make one incredulous. In documenting these acts, photographs would have been able to allay any doubts. One frequently cited extract from one of the letters from German soldiers known to mention the Jews, sent from Tarnopol in early July 1941, is doubtless bursting with eloquence but leaves no doubt about how photography was used as proof:

> So far, we have sent about 1000 Jews into the hereafter, but that is still far too few for what they have done. The Ukrainians have said that the Jews occupied all the leadership positions and regularly have public parties with the Soviets, during which they execute Jews and Ukrainians. I ask you, dear parents, to make this known, you too, father, in the local branch [of the NSDAP]. If there should be any doubts, we will bring photos with us. Then there will be no more doubts.[109]

In November 1941, an order from Chief of the Armed Forces High Command himself, General Keitel, prohibits photographing the execution of Soviets.[110] At the same moment, on the side of the SS, the Reichsführer himself issues the following prohibition to photograph the "executions" that the Einsatzgruppen had been carrying out since the end of June. In this order, Himmler explains that in cases where such shots were needed for reasons of service, all of them had to be given over to the authorities. As is the case for many other documents issued by the Nazi leadership, no copy of this order from the Reichsführer has been found. But direct reference is made to it in the opening of a letter that has survived, written by Heydrich on 16 April 1942 to the chiefs of police and the SS of the occupied territories.[111] The prohibition, it seems, is decidedly difficult to enforce since he suggests that photographs, films, and photographic plates have already been sent to various services in the country (*in Heimat*), that it is therefore necessary to refer this material without delay (*unverzüglich*) to the RSHA, with the heading "Secret Business of the Reich" (*Geheime Reichssache*), and giving the date and location where the shots were taken. What is more, a declaration must be included regarding the honor of the service member who was in possession of them up to that point, attesting that he did not take other photographs and that he has remitted all plates, films, and new prints (*alle Platten, Filme und Abzüge*).[112] In February 1943, Rudolf Hoess, Commandant of Auschwitz, to the SS of the camp: "Recall that it is strictly forbidden to take photographs inside the camp. I will severely punish any infractions."[113] And again on 24 April 1944, Alfred Rosenberg, the Minister of the Reich for the Occupied Territories of the East, sends a note to the Wehrmacht command on the subject of an article published in the *Pravda* six months earlier, on 24 October 1943. This article reported that a photograph "*von der Exekution einer Sowjetagentin*" (of the execution of a Soviet female agent) had been found in the pocket of the uniform of a German officer who had been killed. Having reported this information, Rosenberg asks that the Wehrmacht units be issued strong reminders of the orders prohibiting photography of executions of any kind ("*die Befehle über das Verbot des Fotografierens von Exekutionen jeder Art bei allen Einheiten nachdrücklich in Erinnerung zu bringen*").[114]

*

In the photographs reproduced here, the only witnesses we see are the perpetrators and the victims. We do not see buildings. Only the sand. And the sea in the background.

These photographs were taken at the Baltic seaside.

> Johann Gottfried von Herder:
> Surrounded by German, Slavic, and Finnish nations, the peaceable Lettonian could nowhere extend, still improve, and at length, like its neighbours the Prussians, was most remarkable for the violences which all the inhabitants of these coasts experienced, partly from the new-converted Poles, partly from the Teutonic knights, and those whom they called in to their assistance. Humanity shudders at the blood, that was here spilled in long and savage wars, till the ancient Prussians were nearly extirpated, and the Courlanders and Lettonians reduced to a state of slavery, under the yoke of which they still languish. Centuries perhaps will pass, before it is removed, and these peaceful people are recompensed for the barbarities, with which they were deprived of land and liberty, by being humanely formed anew to the use and enjoyment of an improved freedom.[115]

Writing in the second half of the eighteenth century, Herder could not have known how right he still was almost two centuries later.

Courlanders: inhabitants of the Duchy of Courland. Which, from the mid-sixteenth century to the end of the eighteenth century, covers the western part of present-day Latvia. Founded and directed by the Germans, which is where the name *Kurland* comes from, the land of the Kurs, a Baltic people in ancient times. Which was a province of the Russian Empire throughout the entirety of the nineteenth century. Which was annexed in 1915 by a Germany at war. Slow succession of opposing sovereignties. Until the creation of the three Baltic States in the immediate aftermath of the war.[116] Kurland became Kurzeme (*zeme*: land, in Latvian), one of the administrative regions of the new State. On 27 November 1918, nine days after Latvia declares independence, the first edition of the daily *Kurzemes Wahrds* (The Kurzeme Word) appears. A sign of the maintenance of German influence, the articles, written in Latvian, are, like the title, printed in Gothic script.[117] This daily is published in the capital city of Kurzeme. Called Libau by those for whom German prevails. Liepaja by those who prefer to call it by its Latvian name. The very new independence of these three Republics, which "constituted a type of living topographical bridge between Germany and the Soviet Union," lasted no more than twenty years.[118] The first of the secret clauses of the nonaggression pact signed in August 1939 between Hitler's Germany and Stalin's USSR clarifies in effect that "in the event of a territorial and political rearrangement in the areas belonging to the Baltic States (Finland, Estonia, Latvia, Lithuania), the northern boundary of Lithuania shall represent the boundary of the spheres of influence of German and the U.S.S.R."[119] This "territorial and political rearrangement" did not wait. One year later, in June 1940, Estonia, Latvia, and Lithuania are occupied by Soviet troops and annexed a little later, each of them becoming a Socialist Soviet Republic. The Soviet annexation, in turn, would not last more than a year. On Sunday, 22 June 1941, the first day of Operation Barbarossa, the German army violated the pact signed ten months earlier with Stalin and invaded the territory of the Soviet Union along the entire front from North to South. In the north, Lithuania and then Latvia are first in line. An industrial port, Libau is the westernmost Latvian city on the Baltic. It is also less than a hundred kilometers from the Lithuanian border. As recounted in a diary from the front: "In zwei Tagen durch zwei Länder. Litauen war gestern, heute stehen wir vor Libau" (Two countries in two days. Yesterday Lithuania, today we face Libau).[120] The entirety of Latvia is occupied on 10 July.

The four Einsatzgruppen immediately follow in the wake of the Wehrmacht, then, North and South. Einsatzgruppe A is responsible for the three Baltic countries and a part of Belorussia, or Weißruthenien (White Ruthenia).[121] Composed of 900 men, it is the largest and by far the most effective. The heads of the Einsatzgruppen send the figures for their operations to Berlin. Between November 1941 and January 1942, groups B, C, and D have killed between 45,000 and 95,000 Jews. From the four areas of territory divided into four groups, the area that Einsatzgruppe A is responsible for has the lowest number of Jews in it. But the numbers of those exterminated there are a great deal higher than in the three other groups. The next paragraph speaks of nothing but numbers.

The detailed report that the commander of Einsatzgruppe A, "the fanatical doctor Stahlecker," sends to Berlin in January 1942 gives "the situation as of October 25, 1941" in columns, along with totals and a summary of the number of "executions" completed by that day.¹²² 118,430 Jews and 3,387 Communists, to which the report adds: "Jews liquidated in pogroms," the 748 "executed insane," as well as the Jews and Communists killed along the border region.¹²³ Almost 140,000 men, women, and children killed in four months in the Baltic countries and a part of Belorussia. Among them, in Latvia, 30,000 Jews of about 66,000 who were living there when the Germans arrived. 25,000 more are killed in the city of Riga alone on 30 November and 8 December of that year.¹²⁴ All told, less than 10 percent of the Jews of Latvia are still alive at the end of 1941, and less than 2 percent in 1945, in this country where, after Estonia, their extermination was proportionally highest in Europe.¹²⁵

Are such figures, in such a timespan, more intelligible if one looks at them for one city only?

On 29 June 1941, 7,000 Jews live in Libau.

On 1 July 1942, there are 830.¹²⁶

*

As we know, serious research into the collaboration of local populations with the Nazi occupiers did not come easily or quickly. For this reason, it was often initiated by researchers outside the states where this collaboration occurred.¹²⁷ This issue arises in an even more complex and forceful way in relation to countries where the Nazi occupation was followed by a lengthy period of annexation by the USSR. Not only followed, actually, since the annexation had begun in June 1940 before being interrupted, the following year, by the German invasion. The Soviet annexation resulted in a violent repression, a seizure of goods, mass arrests, and, in the night of 13–14 June 1941, the deportation of 14,000 Latvians to Siberia. Of those deported, 12 percent were Jewish, which is noteworthy since they constituted no more than 5 percent of the general population.¹²⁸ Such a high percentage in no way impeded the persistent effects of Nazi propaganda in Europe, either during the German occupation or during the decades following the war—propaganda that presented the Jews not as victims of the Soviet Union but as its allies and agents who would have kept the reins of power and controlled the secret police during this first annexation.[129]

Only a decade after Latvia gained independence in 1991, public authorities would make recommendations in support of historical research into these successive occupations.[130] In light of the state control exerted over these recommendations and over the general framework in which this research was to be carried out, it is noteworthy that the Occupation was understood as a continuum from 1940 to 1991.[131] On its own, Latvia's new independence obviously could not repair the situation of "ideological overheating" in which the country had existed starting in 1939, "surrounded or occupied by hostile powers."[132] The rejection of and resentment toward the Soviet Union at the end of a half-century of annexation still characterizes the research undertaken both inside and outside the country, and the defensive character of numerous assertions on the subject of the collaboration highlights just how much this two-headed past continues to weigh on a country without a consensual national memory. The need to recognize and acknowledge the nature and extent of the collaboration of auxiliaries with the Nazis also raised the very sensitive question of antisemitism, in particular regarding the respective roles that Nazis and Latvians played in the persecution and extermination of the Jews. Were there really a lot of "non-German volunteers"? And is it true that, "proportionally, the 1,600,000 Latvians took part just as extensively as any other country did in the destruction of the Jews"?[133] Or rather—in this country where antisemitism "still awaits its historian"—is there reason to think that, "just like the issue concerning the exact number of victims of the Nazi occupation, the number of those who participated in the killings will never be known"?[134]

The scope of the research that still needs to be done is in many ways proportional to the ideological clashes that limit it. Notably, the research will have to greatly refine and substantiate the established generalizations on the subject of reparations between a not-negligible percentage of committed but inactive antisemites, a large majority of people who have no opinion, and a small segment of the population who are outraged by the persecutions, among whom a handful of men and women did all they could to help save the Jews, in the name of their convictions and at considerable risk to their own lives. Among the many pitfalls encountered by this history, still largely to be written, is the evidence that the Soviet version of the facts, such as was circulated for almost a half-century, responded more to the needs of propaganda than to the demands of history. Even before the war was over, Moscow had put in place a commission to investigate the crimes of the Nazis and their collaborators. This took the form of more than 5,000 local commissions sitting from 23 August 1944 to 27 July 1946 across the entire territory formerly under German occupation. For example, reported in Libau (Liepaja), the full name of the local commission was nothing less than "Extraordinary investigative commission into the crimes committed by the German Fascist invaders and their collaborators. Report on the crimes of the Fascist German invaders and their collaborators, committed against innocent civilians and Soviet prisoners in the city of Liepaja, SSR [Soviet Socialist Republic] of Latvia." These reports of the "extraordinary commission," which were systematically kept from foreign researchers until 1989, contained important and detailed information not available elsewhere, but they also contained highly inflated figures regarding the number of victims and an often exaggerated denunciation of the role played by Latvians.

A long report from the autumn of 1942 illustrates the immediate proximity of the Soviet and Nazi occupations, not only in terms of the facts but also in terms of the public opinion of the time. Valdemārs Salnais, the Latvian ambassador in Stockholm at the time, describes the German occupation of his country up until 1942. He calls it a "second occupation" in which the swastika replaced the "blood-red flag of communism" and where the "Bolshevik assassins in Moscow were replaced by the masters of the National-Socialist slaves in Berlin." He explains that "if the Baltic peoples have reasons to rejoice at being freed from the Bolsheviks with the help of the Wehrmacht, the Germans on their side had no less reason for being happy and appreciative at finding a population hostile to Bolshevism in the Baltic countries, an active population which could be used not only from behind but also directly up front." He mentions a captain of the Latvian army who seized the premises of the radio station in Riga even before the Germans had arrived in the capital, and reports on the statements made by one of the puppet "General Directors" the Nazis installed at the head of administrations upon their arrival in Latvia. Statements whose vehemence exceeds even the rhetoric expected of an appointed collaborator: "We are the mortal enemies of the Soviet system and the mere thought of a return of Bolshevism, of the Cheka [the secret police], and the Red Army fills us with horror." For his part, Voldemārs Salnais resorts to the word *Asiatic* to denounce the system in his autumn 1942 report; notably, he calls the Soviet occupation of the previous year "the Asiatic terror of the Bolshevik commissars."[135]

Publication of *Kurzemes Vārds*, the daily in Libau, was suspended for the entirety of the Soviet occupation. It began again three days after the Germans entered the city. The paper is printed entirely in Latvian, with the exception of one notice in the two languages right beside the title, beginning with the first issue of 2 July 1941 and signed by the Ostkommandant and Lieutenant Commander Stein, indicating that the text of the paper had been *geprüft und genehmigt*, read and approved, words that both the dictionary and historical context authorize us to translate rather as "inspected and authorized."

The first words of the collaboration are printed on the first page of that first day:

> *Mēs pateicamies slavenajam vadonim Adolfam Hitleram!*
> *Viņa cīņa ir arī mūsu cīņa!*
> We are grateful to the illustrious leader Adolf Hitler!
> His struggle is our struggle![136]

Beginning the very next day, it is no longer the "Commandant of the East and Lieutenant Commander" Stein who gives this authorization, but the Zensuroffizier, whose role is easy to understand without having to be translated. On 9 July, in this very paper, the residents of Libau are called upon to denounce the Jews and the Bolsheviks.[137]

Immediately following the entry of the Germans into Riga, thirty-one-year-old jurist Viktors Arājs puts together a commando of Latvian auxiliaries. Three hundred of his fellow countrymen are now available as killers.[138] In Libau, the massacre of the Jews begins on 29 June, the very day the Wehrmacht enters the city.[139] The women and children are generally spared. The men are arrested. They are killed in a park in the middle of the city, near the lighthouse, at the fishing port, on the naval base. They are killed in Shkede twelve kilometers north of Libau, an uninhabited place, nothing but sand dunes along the Baltic, that the Latvian army had used as a firing range before the war. Unlike what happens in Riga, where Latvian auxiliaries immediately participate in the killings, the Germans from the Einsatzkommando who entered Libau behind the Wehrmacht troops are the main perpetrators until August. During the very early period, the role played by the Latvians in Libau is often to arrest the Jews—they live in the same city, know them, know where they live—and take them to the former women's prison, which serves as a transit point before they are transported to one of the massacre sites.[140]

One episode in particular shows the extent to which it was decidedly not enough for the leaders of the Wehrmacht to leave the massacres in the hands of the Einsatzgruppen and that, at times, they were the ones who gave the order to kill. On 22 July 1941 in the German naval center of Kiel on the Baltic, the commanding admiral registers in the station's log the text of a telegram that was sent to him by the naval commander of Libau, Hans Kawelmacher. Either in an expression of sincere concern or a somewhat exaggerated remark geared toward alarming his superiors, Kawelmacher requests of the commanding admiral of the Baltic Fleet in Kiel about one hundred SS men and fifty Schupo "for a rapid solution to the Jewish problem [*zur schnellen Durchführung Judenproblem*], stating that these men will also be carrying out tasks to maintain public order. Almost 8,000 Jews here. Given the number of SS presently available, the solution to the Jewish problem would take almost a year, which would be inadmissible with regard to the satisfaction [*sic, Befriedigung*] of Libau."[141] Almost a year . . . Luckily, with the Arājs Kommando, one has killers on hand in Riga.

The operations of this commando were extremely well organized, even when they had to take place in areas remote from the capital. About forty armed men would board a Riga city bus, blue in color, well stocked with supplies: vodka, sausages, and cigarettes. The blue bus of the Arājs Kommando would circulate everywhere in Latvia, since there were Jews everywhere. According to a 1935 census, there were 93,000 Jews in the country, but only 7,000 of them lived in rural communities—whereas the large majority of other Latvians were rural. This census had 207 cities listed, according to categories that included even villages with only a few dozen inhabitants. There were Jews living in 158 of these.[142] In some villages, there were simply too few Jews to justify sending the commando's bus to the site, particularly in the province of Vidzeme where there were no more than 2,000 in total. In such cases, Latvian police would facilitate the work of the commando by collecting them together in a larger village so that the commando could then kill as soon as the bus arrived. The same concern for the rationalization and efficiency of the blue bus's itinerary sometimes meant that it would make circuits, stopping at different villages. Of the 21,000 Jews living in Latvia in very small cities before the war, about 15,000 were killed by the men of the Arājs Kommando.

So, on 22 July 1941, a local head of the Kriegsmarine requested from Libau that his superior, based in Kiel, find killers for him. The superior sends the execution order from Kiel to Riga, and a group from the Arājs Kommando immediately leaves for Libau, two hundred kilometers west of the capital. On 27 July 1941, the local chief sends a new telegram to Kiel, clearly less nervous than the earlier one. But still vigilant: "Jewish question in Libau in large part resolved [*größtenteils erledigt*] by execution of almost 1,100 Jewish men by Riga SS Kommando on 24 and 25.7. Kommando SS departed. To finish the remaining work [*Erledigung von Restaufgaben*], the SS Kommando of Libau must remain in place."[143]

The SS Kommando indeed remained in place in Libau. In September, it enlisted a company of Latvian guards, members of the SD. The thirty or so men that make it up are, from that moment on, among the most active killers. The pace of the massacres is much less sustained than in July. It is true that there were fewer and fewer Jewish men still alive. They were killed by the dozen in small shooting actions (*kleinen Erschiessungsaktionen*), as the Germans called them. Then one day in winter, the order arrived from Riga by telegram to accelerate the pace. The pace accelerated. Collaboration between the occupying Germans and the local Latvians had by that point been well established. The first were in charge. Both the Germans and the Latvians generally made up part of one of the commandos of Einsatzgruppe A, specifically Einsatzkommando 2. As for the military, not content with sending telegrams, they participated in the killings on more than one occasion. The list of the formations involved in the extermination of the Jews, in Libau and in the whole of Latvia, is long and heavy: Germans from the SS, the Sicherheitspolizei, and the Sicherheitsdienst, the Ordnungspolizei, and the Wehrmacht; Latvians from the Sicherheitsdienst, the Schutzmannschaft, the national guard, and the army.

Things really did accelerate: over the course of three days, on 15, 16, and 17 December 1941, German and Latvian men would kill more than 2,700 Jews. That is, half of those who were still alive in Libau at the time. A certain number of them at the military port, most of them in the dunes surrounding Shkede.

It is in Shkede that the photographs reproduced at the beginning of the book were taken, on the first of these three days.

This is how it happened.

The articles in the *Kurzemes Vārds* are still in Latvian, with some news in both languages reporting on the successes of the German army on the ground, at sea, and in the air. December comes. Christmas is approaching. An efficient occupier takes care of everything, right down to the smallest details. On page 4 of *Kurzemes Vārds* from the Saturday 13 December 1941 edition, a *Bekanntmachung* (notification) gives the official price scale for the sale of *Weihnachtsbäume* (Christmas trees) depending on their size: "0.40 Reichsmark (RM) per tree up to 1 m.; 0.60 RM up to 1.5 m.; 1 RM from 1.50 m to 2.50 m; 1.40 RM above 2.50m."

And, just below this *Bekanntmachung* about the price of Christmas trees, another one:

Bekanntmachung

des Generalkommisars in Riga vom 10. Dezember 1941 über Verbraucherhöchstpreise für Weihnachtsbäume ab örtlicher Verkaufsstelle im Generalbezirk Lettland.

Gemäss § 3 der Allgemeinen Anordnung über die Preis- und Lohngestaltung im Ostland vom 11. September 1941 setze ich mit dessen Zustimmung folgende Verbraucherhöchstpreise für Weihnachtsbäume ab örtlicher Verkaufsstelle in allen Orten des Generalbezirks Lettland fest:
bis 1 m Höhe 0,40 RM je Stück,
über 1—1,50 m Höhe 0,60 RM je Stück,
über 1,50—2,50 m Höhe 1,— RM je Stück,
über 2,50 m Höhe 1,40 RM je Stück.
Die Preise treten mit dem Tage der Veröffentlichung in Kraft.

Im Auftrage:
gez. Dr. v. B o r c k e.

Bekanntmachung

Juden dürfen am Montag, den 15. Dezember 1941 und am Dienstag, den 16. Dezember 1941 ihre Wohnungen nicht verlassen.

L i b a u, den 12. Dezember 1941.
Der SS- und Polizei-Standortführer Libau,
Dr. Dietrich.

Figure 7. *Kurzemes Vārds*, 13 December 1941.

Translation (bottom article):
Announcement
Jews are not allowed to leave their homes on Monday December 15, 1941 and Tuesday December 16, 1941.
Libau, December 12, 1941.
The Commandant of the SS and the Police Libau,
Dr. Dietrich.

The notifications about the trees and the Jews are also given in Latvian on the same page.[144]

Archival documents do not indicate whether the price scale for Christmas trees was successful or not. As for the Jews, the effectiveness of the order given on that day by Fritz Dietrich, the chief of the Libau police—Dr. Dietrich as he signs and as everyone calls him—is confirmed. By the journal he kept at that time, in which he records the "executions" in Libau, where he has been stationed since the month of September.[145] By the congratulations that he issues to those who took part in them. By the identification of the victims.[146] By the trials: seven German members of the SD who took part in the extermination of the Libau Jews in 1941 and 1942 were sentenced on 14 October 1971 in Hannover;[147] another, Hans Baumgartner, had been sentenced on 18 March of the same year in Berlin, which was then in the German Democratic Republic.[148] The photographs taken on 15 December 1941 in Shkede, eight of which are reproduced here, were presented during these two trials. "This *Aktion*, the so-called 'December *Aktion*,'" states the Hannover verdict, "constituted without doubt a terrifying climax of the extermination of the Jews in Libau."[149]

The order, this time, is no longer limited to the arrests of men. Without waiting for the Monday specified in the 12 December 1941 issue of *Kurzemes Vārds*, the Latvian police begins to clear out the Jewish families from their homes during the night of Saturday to Sunday and take them to the former women's prison that is being used as a transit site between the roundup and the murders. The pace picks up the next day. Beginning at four in the morning. "Entire columns of Jewish citizens, the elderly, the weak, pregnant women, and mothers with infants were pulled from their homes by Latvian police and taken to the prison." In the course of the roundup, they are confined to the courtyard of this prison, which is much too small to contain all those arriving. *Auf diesem Hof herrschte einfach die Hölle*, in this courtyard, it was simply hell, as the Hannover verdict puts it. They are ordered to face the wall, but there is not enough wall for so many faces. The noise is deafening, *ein ohrenbetäubender Lärm*, the people piled in are moaning and screaming, the little ones cry, the mothers let their despair burst out as they face the imminent end of their children, *das bevorstehende Ende ihrer Kinder*.[150] So the Latvian police and the German SD assigned to the prison begin to beat. The same scenes of distress and terror are repeated on Monday, Tuesday, and Wednesday. So they beat in the yard on Monday, Tuesday, and Wednesday. They beat those in front of the prison who refuse to get into the military trucks covered with tarps and pulled up to the prison gate. They pile them in. The smallest children are grabbed by an arm or a leg and tossed in.[151] A first transport leaves for Shkede on Sunday evening. The people rounded up are guarded for the whole night—is it even possible to imagine this night?—in a large wooden stable, which the Latvian army had used on its firing range before the war. Monday, the trucks are in full swing in continuous shifts between the city and the dunes. From the houses to the prison, from the prison to Shkede. Only the trucks returning from the dunes roll empty. On the Tuesday and Wednesday of these winter days, many are forced to walk on foot the dozen kilometers between the city and the dunes.

In the days before, no one in Libau knew why members of the Latvian police were being outfitted with shovels and taken by truck northward, which is the direction of Shkede. Rumors circulated, perhaps started by the occupiers, that it was to build *Befestigungsanlagen*, fortifications, in case the Soviets invaded from the Baltic Sea. Fortifications in the sand, dug with shovels. . . . This was not a defense structure but, one kilometer from the road, a pit they had dug in the Shkede dunes. A pit that was long, large, and deep, running parallel to the sea.[152] Some twenty members of the Latvian guard from Libau received an order on Sunday, 14 December, from their lieutenant to present themselves at 5:30 the next morning in the barracks. From there they were taken to Shkede, their covered truck following a car carrying the German commanders. Like workmen leaving for a construction site. They could not aim, since the sun is not up and it is winter; they will therefore not begin shooting before 8:00 a.m. So the killers have plenty of time to get ready. They kill for three whole days, literally from morning to evening. The process is established with a view to the greatest efficiency, each step in the sequence taking place at its precise location. Ideally, each sequence should be carried out at a pace such that each step would neither slow down nor rush the steps before or after. They did their best to establish this ideal rhythm. As soon as a truck from the prison arrives in Shkede, the people who had been shoved, thrown in are made to get out. They do the same with those who, forced to leave the prison, walked as they were able the twelve kilometers along the road, snow-covered or slippery when the temperature had risen a little. They are held in the large stable. They are made to leave in groups of twenty and move toward the dune. To lie face down on the frozen sand, about fifty meters from the pit that had been dug. They are made to get up, in groups of ten. Made to get undressed because it is their turn to be killed. To move forward to the edge of the pit.

Trucks will come to collect the clothes left on the sand. They will be piled up, they will be useful. The pieces of white cloth in the pit resemble shrouds and without any possible hope that any body would have had the time to protect itself by itself at the moment when it was still alive.

> A story translated from American, *The Shawl* by Cynthia Ozick... revolves around a baby, Magda. Thus we know it is a fiction since a Jewish baby, in an extermination camp, is by definition dead. (But there could be a fleeting exception here or there: a hidden Jewish baby.) Magda is wrapped in a shawl, absolute necessity but also a transitional object.... "Stella, cold, cold, the coldness of hell. How they walked on the roads together, Rosa with Magda curled up between sore breasts, Magda wound up in the shawl. Sometimes Stella carried Magda. But she was jealous of Magda. A thin girl of fourteen, too small, with thin breasts of her own, Stella wanted to be wrapped in a shawl, hidden away, asleep, rocked by the march, a baby, a round infant in arms. Magda took Rosa's nipple, and Rosa never stopped walking, a walking cradle...."[153] Rosa, clinging to it, will bring the shawl back. She will not bring Magda back. Stella will remain cold. All of us there [at the Auschwitz-Birkenau camp] were—I was—Magda, Stella, Rosa at the same time. Even if the shawl were empty, even if there were no shawl at all, that only our skin remained, wrapping an increasingly light burden. I remember an almost hallucinatory bodily experience. Very sick, with a high fever, I had gone to the *Revier* [hospital barracks], in spite of the risk of being selected for the gas chamber. In the meantime, at least I could remain lying down and not go to work. Since I had been fairly athletic before, my back seemed able to cope better than the rest of me. And lying, huddled up on the side, I had the feverish sensation of being in the refuge of my own

back that maternally curved around me. When I was not delirious, I was thinking: I must bring me back to them. I had to bring back me, what remained of this piece of her, of the flesh of her flesh, to my mother. It was a real duty that I felt. But I do not think it was along the lines of a "you will love yourself like your neighbor." Rather more, *I* had to bully this *me* who only wanted to slide, to bully it to return to life, to her.[154]

At least in the photographs reproduced here, one can read that not every victim received the same order. Only the youngest women, it seems, were made to strip naked. But these photographs do not say what arbitrariness, what degree of voyeurism, sadism, disgust, or indifference produced these variations in the order to undress, partially or totally, given by the murderers who, before killing them, look at these women and these young girls, each forced to undress beside the woman who conceived her, beside the woman to whom she gave life, in such a bitterly cold winter that those who come forward, already naked, join arms, not to shield their sex from the murderous gazes but to protect themselves against the cold in a gesture of ultimate survival. These photographs do not say whether, even for a moment, there appeared in the minds of the murderers standing in front of the elderly women even a trace of the fear or respect they would have had for the bodies of their own mothers. Or if in the minds of the murderers standing in front of the children there appeared even the slightest reminder of their own children's bodies. These photographs do not say whether the people trembling from cold, terror, and total abandonment, and whom the murderers are watching as they undress, run, and die—whether in their murderers' eyes, these people have even the remotest connection to "the sphere of human obligation and responsibility," or whether the murderers do not have for a single instant "the feeling of belonging to the same humanity as their victims."[155] They also do not say what these three women and this very young girl are experiencing, forced to pose in front of the camera before dying. And the little one in the white bonnet, whose face we cannot see. We do not hear whether she is crying. Nor do these photographs say whether, as unthinkable as this is (but is it even possible to think such a moment?), it is an automatic gesture that moves one of them to raise her hand up to her hair. Or whether it is the human being behind the camera—since it is a human being—who ordered her to make this gesture, perhaps to make the shot seem more composed.[156] This woman no longer exists, but the movement of her hand remains. Questioning about the origins of this gesture is specific to every look that manages to land on this scene. As is the interrogation of what the least suffocating of hypotheses may be.

Libau is a protected port because the Baltic does not freeze at this spot. Located just a few minutes from the city center is an immense white sand beach accessible through small dunes. Before the war, families often go to the seaside, *am Strand*, as soon as the weather permits. All summer, even when the weather is less nice. Every day. Until the weather no longer permits it, sometime in the autumn. Libau belongs to the sea, and the sea belongs to Libau. The sand, the waves. And the breeze—constant. "Atme, frische Luft!" (Breathe, fresh air!), said the mothers. It is even Libau's nickname: "the city where the wind was born." Is it possible to imagine what violence it entails that this very seaside spot—so familiar, so familial, so much a part of everyday life—this very sand of their childhood, is where the children, teenagers, and women in the photographs reproduced here are going to be killed? The place where they lived, where they experienced their greatest joys, becomes the very site of their death.

In winter in Libau the wind is no longer a breeze. It heaves violently onto the dunes. In one of the photographs we see how, crashing in from the sea, it whips and thrashes the hair and the clothes that remain on the bodies of a few silhouettes advancing against this wind, behind the young boy who has his head turned toward the photographer. Would we know in what direction this strange column of people is heading, legs all bent, if we did not already know? And, if we did not already know, what of the nine women standing, one of them bent over, backs turned, and whose eyes we cannot see—who is looking at the sea and who has closed her eyes as her last line of defense? If we did not already know, would the immobility of their bodies suggest that they are living their very last moments? In the photograph where they are standing with their backs to their murderers, the only thing we see of the pit is the narrow band of sand on which they are standing. Even if we do not know, we know why it is that human beings—here again, human beings—have come up with the idea to shape this rim on the interior of the pit.

After each salvo from the other side of the pit, hierarchy required that a German from the Sicherheitsdienst move forward to give the *Gnadenschuss* (*coup de grâce*) with his service weapon to victims that the round of bullets had not managed to kill. The pit was filling up. However, some bodies became stuck on this interior slope perhaps because, being younger, they were lighter and the sand held them back. So one man is assigned a very specific job. In the last of the photographs reproduced here, this man who walks carrying a stick in his right hand—he was probably right-handed—and who uses the stick to help get the dead bodies to rejoin those who are lying in the pit, this man walking in his military coat, whose step seems slow and quiet, is he thinking?

His uniform indicates that it is a Latvian who has been assigned this task that has no name, but nonetheless exists since it is shown in the process of being fulfilled. Who is showing it? In all these photographs, only men in Latvian uniform are visible—uniforms of the police and of the Latvian members of the SD. The Germans are not in the photographs. They are the photographers. As murderer-witnesses, they are watching and getting on film what they are in the process of carrying out. The image is perpetrated by them just as the murder itself is perpetrated by them. It is because they are killing that the executioners will first photograph the victims. While they avoid being seen by those who will later see the photographs, the amusing idea sometimes occurs to them to force these women and this girl—who will all be killed on their orders a moment later—to look at them.

The concrete methods the persecutors used to put the persecution into images varied, depending on the locations and the circumstances. A young member of the Ordnungspolizei posing, all smiles, beside humiliated Jews, still alive but already among the hunted from the mere fact of having suffered this humiliation.[157] But then among the hunted for real when dead Jews become "trophies," photographed, preserved, sent to families—so strong are the pride or the enjoyment they seem to provide to the murderers, despite repeated orders forbidding them from taking photographs, keeping them, or sending them.

Other exigencies sometimes determined the methods of capturing images. This time, a political exigency. In Shkede, on 15 December 1941, the Germans are standing outside the frame. The Jews are the victims; the Latvians the murderers. Allegedly, the Germans are only witnesses. Their conspicuous absence from the photographs reproduced here will be extensively commented upon after the war, amongst the population and during the trial when murderers and witnesses, brought together as the accused, will try very hard to exculpate themselves.[158] Later still, the responsibility of the Latvian collaborators for the Nazi crimes in the country as a whole will require historical research and, at the same time, hinder it. These commentaries, accusations, and research will feed on what was said and written during the war itself. In terms that clearly express the point of the propaganda, the Commander of Einsatzgruppe A, Stahlecker, explained in his general report on the activities of the group up to the autumn of 1941 that in Riga his men had taken some photographs and made films of some *Selbstreinigungsaktionen*, which were to serve "as evidence for later times of the violence of the local population against the Jews."[159] Another one of these German compound words the Nazis used so much—*Selbst*: self; *Reinigung*: cleansing. Actions of self-cleansing, then.

In Libau, there are no spontaneous or incited pogroms. The operations were carried out in an organized way: first by the Germans alone, then by the Arājs Kommando in July, and, beginning in the following month, by the Latvian members of the SD, recruited on site, who reported to the SS. On unequal terms, the Germans and the Latvians were already shifting the burden of responsibility for the massacres onto one another. A passage from the report sent to the commander of the Ordnungspolizei in Riga, two weeks after the *Dezember-Aktion* in Shkede, by the chief of the Libau police, Dr. Dietrich, testifies to this. A report consisting of six pages and twelve points. From 1, *Allgemeine Lage* (general situation), to 12, *Stimmung der Truppe* (troop morale). The response to point 12 is quick and simple: "troop morale is good." Return to point 1: describing the atmosphere in the city, Dr. Dietrich speaks of a rumor circulating that this execution had been photographed to show that *"nicht Deutsche, sondern Letten die Erschießung vorgenommen hätten,"* that it was not the Germans but the Latvians who would have done the killing.[160] Since the last report, dated 13 December, there has been no substantial change in the political situation, there was no action undertaken by *kommunistische Elemente*, three shots fired at a soldier from the Wehrmacht missed their target (those responsible have yet to be found), and the population of Libau is *ruhig* (calm). But, the chief of police explains, the execution of Jews carried out since the last report on the 13th is still the topic of conversation among the local population. The loss of the Jews is often deplored, and thus far, few voices have been heard in favor (*wenig positive Stimmen*) of their elimination.[161] Having given the numerical result of the "executions" carried out in Shkede during the three days—2,772 people, of whom 23 were Communists and 2,749 were Jewish—Dr. Dietrich adds: *"Die Gesamtzahl der noch hier lebenden Juden kann erst nach einer demnächst stattfindenden Registrierung angegeben werden"* (The total number of living Jews still here will be communicated following a process of registration to be carried out soon).

During those three days, the *Erschiessungskommandos* (execution commandos) worked in shifts. Shift rotations took place after ten series of ten victims. On Monday, the temperature at the warmest part of the day did not get above 5 degrees Celsius. On Tuesday and Wednesday, it only got to 0 degrees. The Germans had provided coffee spiked with cognac for themselves, the Latvians received their schnapps in bottles. The killing went on without stopping during these three days, until about six o'clock in the evening. Had it been summer, they could have kept going, but in winter there was not enough daylight. And this, which must still be said: "Mothers who were carrying in their arms their *Kleinkinder*"—a tender compound word in German, meaning "babies," "little ones"—"were ordered to raise them above their shoulders and the *Kleinkinder* were executed *zusammen*—together—with their mothers."[162] The torture and the suffering, *Qualen und Leiden*, inflicted on the victims during the three days of this *Aktion* in the month of December 1941 in the Shkede dunes were, the Hannover judgment states, *in menschlich kaum vorstellbarer Weise*, of a kind that is hardly humanly imaginable.¹⁶³

It would have taken too long to throw sand into the pit after murdering each group of ten people: they waited until the end of each day to cover the *in die Grube gestürzten Leichen*, the corpses thrown into the pit. The verb *stürzen* has a number of different meanings, many of which—plunge, topple, lob— could also describe what happened to each of these people. This same verb is used when one has *jemanden ins Unglück gestürzt*, made someone fall into misfortune. *Der Stürmer* had bellowed and plastered "Die Juden sind unser Unglück!" ("The Jews are our misfortune!") everywhere throughout these years.¹⁶⁴ With their corpses being thrown into the pits dug out in so many Shkedes on the immense invaded territory, it was, at last, the Jews' turn to fall into misfortune.

Dr. Dietrich, Libau's police chief, who had prohibited Jews from leaving their homes on 15 and 16 December 1941, was no ingrate. And Christmas time had finally come. On 23 December, he expressed his satisfaction over the obtained result with a gift—perhaps also following instructions on the importance of moments of respite and celebration for the morale of the troops: "The battalion has carried out a difficult service during the period of December 14–17, for which I express all my thanks to the officers and policemen who participated. For this reason, I am granting a leave of three days to each officer and each policeman."¹⁶⁵

*

The photographs from the Shkede *Dezember-Aktion*, eight of which are reproduced here, were presented in sequence at the trials held in 1971 in Berlin and Hannover. They had probably been taken by one of those accused in Hannover, SS-Oberscharführer Carl-Emil Strott, member of the German SD in Libau from July 1941 until the end of 1944.¹⁶⁶ During the 1964 trial of another SS-man, Wolfgang Kügler, Strott was issued a subpoena in Wiesbaden where he was working as a hotel manager. He was sixty-one at the time. In effect, Strott was Kügler's deputy in Libau, where Kügler had been the head of the SD from July 1941 to April 1943. The series of lies, denials, and self-contradictions that Strott voiced during this summons in 1964 is a true model of the genre as it was practiced at the time of their trials by many other members of the SS: they did nothing at all and, at the same time, were only doing their duty. From then on, this self-portrait of the man who does not remember, was not there, was there but saw nothing, did nothing, photographed nothing, constitutes the most conspicuous representation there is of what had been done.[167]

Wiesbaden, January 14th, 1964. Carl-Emil Strott, verbatim [extracts]:

One day I noticed that a commando called Arays [Arājs] was in the city and that clothing was falling out of the commando's trucks, driven by the Latvians. I learned that they were goods belonging to Jews who had been shot.

As I declared earlier, I did the bridge duty three times. Each time I was assigned there by Kügler. The first time, as I learned afterward, Jews had been shot nearby. Guards 2 and 3 had absolutely nothing to do with the execution of Jews. When it was, I cannot say. In any case, Kügler kept me away from it. Along with a few Latvians, my role was to block the access roads to the execution terrain. That is, we were supposed to prevent there from being possible German or native spectators. It was explicitly stated that the executions were not to be made public.

In the instructions that I received, it was not said to me that my role also involved stopping Jews who might try to run away. Incidentally, from that post, I did not see any Jews running away. The first time I arrived at the execution site, the Jews to be executed [*die zu erschießenden Juden*] were already near the execution site. The first time, I'd say that there were between 200 and 300 people (women, men, children).

The execution was carried out by Latvian killers. The victims had to undress and were shot in the back. What I am describing here, I could see from the barricade post where I was.

That Kügler had been present is deduced from the order that he gave to me, in compliance with an order from the Reichsführer, to go and view the corpses from close-up [*daß er mir gemäß einem Reichführerbefehl den Befehl gab, die Leichen von nahe anzusehen*]. So I approached the pit and I saw the victims lying there.

PROSECUTOR [*Staatsanwalt*]: Were you not aware of the numerous other executions of Jews, in particular those near the Libau lighthouse, which was in the immediate vicinity of your office, in the course of which it happened that a thousand people were killed?

STROTT: In effect, I heard talk of many executions of Jews, from Kügler, from colleagues and from the comments of the population that I had to record in my reports on the general atmosphere [*durch Äußerungen der Bevölkerung, die ich für meine Stimmungsberichte einzuholen hatte*]. That a thousand people had been executed, however, I hadn't heard. What I did hear was that the killers were Latvian. My job during these executions was to ensure that everything went smoothly and without complications [*glatt und ohne Schwierigkeiten*]. I know that sounds odd, but I cannot think of any other word at the moment. My colleagues had been assigned this task by Kügler. There were not many discussions on the subject of these *Aktionen* because it had to be kept secret from the Jews and the Latvians. If the information had gotten out regarding the aim [of these *Aktionen*], that could have created difficulties [*Schwierigkeiten*].

PROSECUTOR: Witnesses . . . reported that before the *Aktion* of February 1942, they heard you say in effect that there were still too many Jews. They said that you had played, alongside Kügler, the principle role in the Libau executions. In December 1941, you are said to have given clothing stained with blood to the Jewish cleaning lady in your service.

STROTT: I maintain that it is impossible for me to have expressed myself in that way or to have done that [*Ich halte es für unmöglich, daß ich mich so geäußern und so verhalten habe*].

PROSECUTOR: Did you yourself take photographs of the Libau executions, or did you have such photographs taken?

STROTT: No, but I know that such photographs were taken.

The photographs, eight of which are reproduced here, were then presented.

STROTT: These images, I did not take them, I do not know anything about them. I do not recognize anything at all about where they were taken either.

PROSECUTOR: You took part on many occasions in what you call *Absperrungen* [roadblocks], even though you obviously knew that human beings were killed solely because of their belonging to a particular race [*Rassenzugehörigkeit*].

STROTT: Many times, I wanted to get away from this "heap."[168] I did not succeed. At the time, I did not do this with joy, and I also found that these activities were not correct [*nicht in Ordnung*]. But I had taken an oath and I thought that for my country I had to obey every order.

Carl-Emil Strott's self-portrait before the German courts did not change during the seven years between this 1964 summons and his own trial. In fact, in 1971, before the Hannover court, he stated that "in the General SS,[169] I was never told that the Jews were inferior persons [*minderwertige Menschen*] and that they had to be removed [*vernichtet werden müssten*]. Only later, in Libau, did this become clear to me for the first time [*dies wurde mir erst nachher in Libau klar*]. Kügler said it. Inwardly, I objected to the extermination. Truth be told, I did not ask myself the question of why."[170]

Among the seven counts of accessory to mass murder (*Beihilfe zum gemeinschaftlichen Mord*) in the indictment against Carl-Emil Strott, the Hannover court accepted the surveillance of the bridges, but not in the terms given by the accused, because at least two hundred Jews had been struck down there. It accepted the roadblock, but not in the terms given by the accused, because at least twenty Jews had been struck down there. It accepted the fact that Strott had approached the edge of the pit but, the judgment states, the accused did not only see the bodies, as he had claimed, but had killed at least fifty Jews who were not yet dead. Finally, the court found him guilty of complicity in the murder of more than 2,700 Jews killed in Shkede in 1941 during this *Dezember-Aktion*.[171]

*

A dead Jew is of no use. Other than being dead, which was precisely the mission of the SS and which the Einsatzgruppen had carried out so well as of June 1941. But another logic would suggest that a Jew kept alive was a useable Jew. By giving them just enough food to keep them alive, the Jews could actually be exploited as a workforce, in particular the technicians and craftspeople. For a time, these two logics place the civil administration and the SS in opposition at the highest levels. What's more, the former was concerned with maintaining room to manoeuver while faced with the hegemony of the latter. Although the chief civilian administrator for the Ostland,[172] Reichskommissar Hinrich Lohse, never loses sight of the final aim that is elimination, the "preliminary guidelines for the treatment of the Jews" that he presents to the Higher SS and Police on 4 August 1941, on top of registration, labeling, and expropriation, include concentration into ghettos and forced labor.[173] The reaction of Stahlecker, Commandant of Einsatzkommando A, is shown in a long and irritated, increasingly hysterical memo dated 6 August. In this document, he denounces the measures proposed by Lohse, which, he says, have not taken into account an essential given: the fact that, for the first time, a radical treatment of the Jewish question is possible in the East (*die im Ostraum erstmalig mögliche radikale Behandlung der Judenfrage*). In any case, he adds, given the number of non-Jewish workers who had been returned to jobs that had been stolen from them by the Jews and the Bolsheviks, no Jewish workers were needed. These latter are very often Communist activists and saboteurs who sow disorder and, given the urgent need to pacify the East, all sources of disorder must be eliminated.

To say nothing of the fact that the consequence of maintaining Jews in the largest cities would be their continuing existence as parasites. Moreover, continues Stahlecker in his scathing SS response to the economic considerations of the civil administration, the fact is that, even in the capital of the Reich, despite measures undertaken by the state and the party, still in 1941 Jews were managing to pass as Aryans and to practice *Rassenmischung* (racial mixing). The risk of having Jewish blood spread through *Rassenmischung* therefore should not be underestimated. Particularly in the Baltic countries, where the racially valuable segment of the population must be protected from such mixing. For that to happen, the fertility of the Jews must be limited by any means possible and as quickly as possible. Sterilization being impracticable, the only solution is to physically separate the two sexes.[174] To that end, "Jewish reservation areas" (*Judenreservatsräume*) will be established in which boys shall remain with their mothers until they have reached the age of sexual maturity. Jews will be immediately placed into forced labor, inside and outside the areas.

In summary, concludes Stahlecker, the Jewish question shall be resolved: first, through the immediate and total expulsion of Jews from the eastern territories; second, by preventing Jews from increasing in number; third, by utilizing them to the maximum possible degree as a work force; fourth, in facilitating to the extent possible the transfer of the Jews to a reservation area situated outside Europe. He then adds a handwritten recommendation, at the bottom of this long, typed memorandum in which he has laid out, in black and white, his opinion and suggestions with a view to the best possible resolution of the Jewish question: "I consider it desirable, before issuing any basic statement, once more to discuss these questions verbally, especially since it is safer that way, and since it concerns fundamental orders from higher authority to the Security Police, ones that should not be discussed in writing. *Brigadefuhrer.*"[175]

In the autumn of this same year, 1941, the disagreements and rivalries between the SS and the civil administration would come up again, at the same high level but on a much smaller scale. Three letters were exchanged between the Reich Minister for the Occupied Eastern Territories and his representative in Riga, Hinrich Lohse, leader of this civil administration for the Ostland. The first very brief letter communicated a complaint from the RSHA, the Reich Security Main Office, from Berlin to Riga. The response from Riga gave explanations and asked for orders. The third letter, from Berlin to Riga again, knew how to put an end to the discussion by recalling both the priorities and the hierarchies.[176]

First letter. Berlin, 31 October 1941. George Leibrandt, Head of the Political Department for the Ministry for the Occupied Eastern Territories, to Hinrich Lohse, Reich Commissioner for the Ostland in Riga.

The Reich Security Main Office has complained that the Reich Commissioner for the Ostland has forbidden execution of Jews in Libau. I request a report in regard to this matter by return mail.

Second letter. Riga, 15 November 1941. Lohse, Reich Commissioner for the Ostland, to the Ministry for the Occupied Eastern Territory in Berlin.

I have forbidden the wild execution of Jews [*die wilde Judenexecutionen*] in Libau because they were not justifiable in the manner in which they were carried out [*sie in der Art ihrer Durchführung nicht zu verantworten waren*].

I should like to be informed whether your inquiry of October 31 is to be regarded as a directive [*dahinhehende Weisung*] that all Jews in the Ostland must be liquidated [*liquidiert*]. Shall this take place without regard to age and sex and economic interests (for instance those of the Wehrmacht for workers qualified in the armament industry)? Of course [selbstverständlich], the cleansing [Reinigung] of the Ostland of Jews is a main task [eine vordringliche Aufgabe]. Its solution, however, must be harmonized with the necessities of war production. . . .[177]

Third letter. Berlin, 18 December 1941. Otto Bräutigam, Joint Head of the Political Department in the Ministry for the Occupied Eastern Territories, to the Reich Commissioner in Riga.

Clarification of the Jewish question has most likely been achieved by now through verbal discussions. Economic considerations should essentially not be taken into account in settling this problem. Moreover, it is requested that questions arising be settled directly with the Higher SS and Police Leader. By order (signed), Bräutigam.

"This declaration ended the incipient struggle for the preservation of the Jewish labor force. The commissioners were now resigned to its loss."[178] In any case, on site, no one had waited for the response from Berlin, the facts having shown what the order of priorities was and who was really making the decisions. Bräutigam's response is dated 18 December 1941. The Shkede *Aktion* had been shut down the night before.

After the Arājs Kommando had come in July, the occupiers worried that if they continued to kill men, they would not have enough much-needed cobblers, electricians, photographers, or tailors, since, as elsewhere, these professions were mainly practiced in Libau by Jews. So, they spared the lives of roughly 350 Jews who were made to perform forced labor, and a certain number of whom were stationed in the basement of the large building where the German SD had established its quarters. But they also had to spare the lives of their immediate family members. They could not expect to get much out of a man who had already lost so many aunts and uncles, cousins, and friends from their school days and adulthood, if they also killed his parents, his brothers and sisters, his wife, and his children.

The initiatives that Einsatzkommando 2 undertook in Libau on this matter were the same as those carried out elsewhere in

Latvia. Or in Lithuania, as is shown by a nine-page report from 1 December 1941 sent from Kauen (Kaunas), the "Jäger report," from the name of its signatory Karl Jäger, the head of Einsatzkommando 3. This typed report, with subtotals reported from page to page, detailed by day, by city (large or small), by sex, by age (old or young), kept track of the Jews "executed" by members of the commando in Lithuania between 2 July and 1 December 1941. An example will suffice: "28.8.41 Joniskia [Joniskis] 47 Jewish men, 165 Jewish women, 143 Jewish children." Page six of the report ends with the total number of "executions": 137,346. Page seven begins with a summary of what this number facilitates for SS-Standartenführer Jäger: *"Ich kann heute feststellen, dass das Ziel, das Judenproblem für Litauen zu lösen, vom EK. 3 erreicht worden ist. In Litauen gibt es keine Juden mehr, ausser den Arbeitsjuden incl. ihrer Familien"* (I can confirm today that the goal of solving the Jewish problem in Lithuania has been reached by the EK [Einsatzkommando] 3. There are no Jews remaining in Lithuania, apart from the Jews forced to work, including their families).[179]

Jews forced to work, including their families, these survivors of Libau, had no idea how long they would survive. The killing continued. At a slower pace, by force of circumstances. There were no longer many Jews alive since the December *Aktion*. Another fifty were killed in Shkede at the beginning of February 1942.[180] And, in this vertiginous absence of the others, of almost all the others, the few Jewish survivors of Libau also had to survive, mentally, the fact of having survived.

David Siwzon is an electrician. He was kept alive. His father died before the war; his brothers and sisters no longer lived in Latvia; he had no children. His mother and his wife were kept alive. One day in 1942—he is twenty-eight years old—when he is in the basement of the building of the SD, he receives the order to go up one floor to do a repair. The office where the electrical installation is broken is that of Carl-Emil Strott, the SS-man-turned-hotel-manager who had done nothing and only his duty. The office is empty. In a half-opened drawer, David Siwzon notices several film negatives. They are already developed, and all he has to do is hold one of them up to the light for a second to know what they show. In among the rest, perhaps Strott will not notice the temporary absence of a roll of film. There is nobody in the corridor. David Siwzon goes back down to the basement where another survivor is working, his friend Meir Stein, who is assigned to the photography laboratory that the SS, who indeed loved photography, had installed there. He leaves the roll with his friend so that he can make copies without being caught. Later, under the pretext of needing to do an additional electrical repair in Strott's office, David Siwzon returns the roll to the drawer. In a corner of the stable behind the SD building, he buries a metal box containing the prints of the photographs, eight of which are reproduced here.

Meir Stein was killed. David Siwzon numbered among the ca. 830 Jews of Libau still alive on 1 July 1942.[181] On that day, they were rounded-up into a ghetto, eleven houses on four streets. They lived there until autumn of the next year, only leaving to go to the places where they worked. On 3 October, David Siwzon, his wife, and two other young adults would escape from the ghetto. Five days later, it was "liquidated" and the approximately 800 people still living there—few were killed in the ghetto—were transported to the Kaiserwald concentration camp near Riga. Most of them were killed on the spot. The oldest and the youngest were deported to Auschwitz. In 1944, the 350 Jews from Libau who were still alive in Kaiserwald were sent to the Stutthof camp in Germany.[182] Approximately 200 of them would survive. To that 200, we must add another eleven people, including David Siwzon, who lived hidden in a Libau basement from October 1943 to the end of the war where they were assisted by a couple of young Latvians who put their own lives at risk for that entire period.[183]

When the Red Army enters the city in May 1945 and the eleven Jews still alive in Libau are able to see the light of day again after nineteen months spent in the basement, David Siwzon goes and digs up the metal box behind the SD building. He hands over the box to a Soviet officer, the box containing the photographs taken on 15 December 1941 in the Shkede dunes, eight of which are reproduced here.

These photographs were taken to Moscow and kept in the USSR archives (later the State Archives of the Russian Federation), where Gerhard Schoenberner would discover them in 1959. Each one has a long caption typed in Russian on the back.[184] Some of them identify the names of those we see in the photographs. And the close family ties between them, since people were amassed together, transported together, killed together. These names are of no interest to the reader here. Besides, to state their names would be to abandon the others, all the others, without identity.

These captions were written in an altogether Soviet style.

> Before shooting them, the German fascist occupiers force the condemned to remove their clothing.

> The German fascist occupiers march naked women to the place where they will be shot.

> Group of women and children lined up near a ditch by their fascist German captors before being shot.

> The German fascist occupiers march the women and children, *mirnie grazhdanie*, to the place where they will be shot.

The other captions do not say anything different. What is written on the back of these photographs gives no indication that these women and children, these *mirnie grazhdanie*—peaceful citizens, that is, noncombatants in wartime—are also Jewish, and that it is for this reason that they have been killed. Twenty-five years later, at the trial in Berlin, the identity of the victims is more explicit. In German this time, but always in the same language: the Jews there are *Sowietbürger*, Soviet citizens, sometimes with the further designation of *Sowjetbürger jüdischer Herkunft*, Soviet citizens of Jewish origin.[185]

In 1971, thirty years after the *Dezember-Aktion* in Shkede, David Siwzon gets permission to leave Latvia to go to Berlin and then to Hannover to testify at the two trials where these photographs were presented. The crimes were the same. Not the tribunals. Hans Baumgartner, the man judged in East Berlin, was sentenced to death and executed. For the defendants in Hannover, the punishments would range from eighteen months to six years in prison. And seven years for Carl-Emil Strott, who had had to wait to be in Libau, where he had done nothing and only his duty, before finding out that Jews were inferior beings. The severity of the Berlin verdict does not make the mildness of the one in Hannover more easily acceptable. And vice-versa.

To shoot. In English, a single verb would have been sufficient to capture the two sequences. They were photographed and then they were killed. These photographs were taken. Were rescued. Were archived. Were discovered. Were produced as evidence during trials. Were reproduced in books, films, museums, temporary exhibitions, or on Internet sites that speak about this death-in-action.

This book opened with a question: To whom do these photographs belong? At the end of the book, will it be considered naive to find it obscene that the photographs reproduced here, along with all the others that speak of the world's suffering, could be withheld? And that the law requires them to bear the stamp of this withholding for decades before granting permission to reproduce them, either through the high- or low-stakes financial transaction it imposes or through a "kind permission"? It is these photographs themselves and not just their *copyright* that belong to the *public domain*.[186] That is, to humanity as a whole. To history.

For me, they also belong to another history: David Siwzon, who was born in Libau on 29 May 1914 and died there on 18 June 1983, was my mother's youngest brother.

Notes

1. Yitzhak Arad, ed., *The Pictorial History of the Holocaust* (New York: Macmillan, 1990).
2. http://motlc.learningcenter.wiesenthal.org.
3. http://www.ushmm.org. The uncertainty of the rules pertaining to copyright or their application can be quite striking at times, raising moral concerns. The self-attribution of copyright by institutions sometimes creates tensions between them, however temporarily. The right to reproduce these eight photographs was requested of the USHMM on 1 July 2008 for the French edition of this book. The "use agreement" received on the 9th in response to that request was followed by a courteous but seemingly somewhat embarrassed email from the same sender on the 10th, indicating that the pho-

tographs were in fact under "exclusive copyright" of the German archives (Bundesarchiv). The USHMM was no longer authorized to give permission for their reproduction. So, requests had to be made to the German archives for permission to reproduce these photos. To my request for clarification regarding the somewhat mysterious events that had arisen between the 9th and 10th of July, I was told by Klaus-Dieter Postupa of the Bundesarchiv's Central Assistance office, Koblenz, that the USHMM was not allowed to designate these photos "Copyright: Public domain" on its website. That in so doing, the USHMM had "disregarded" its agreement with the Bundesarchiv and was in "breach of the rules." The museum had been "requested to correct the information." The USHMM complied, in a quite radical way since the photos themselves disappeared from the public USHMM site.

4. http://www.masada2000.org/holocaust.html. This link is no longer active.
5. On the production and reception of the film, see Sylvie Lindeperg's *"Nuit et brouillard." Un film dans l'histoire* (Paris: Odile Jacob, 2007). I have relied on this work for the facts regarding the presence of this film at Adolf Eichmann's trial in 1961.
6. Jean Cayrol (1911–2005) was a writer (he received the Renaudot Prize in 1947 for the first volume of his fictional trilogy *Je vivrai l'amour des autres*) and, beginning in 1949, an editor at Éditions du Seuil. Cayrol had joined the Resistance very early on and was deported to the Mauthausen concentration camp in March 1943. His first collection of poetry is entitled *Poèmes de la nuit et du brouillard* (Paris: Pierre Seghers, 1946).
7. The sentence "Those on the right" does not continue. Hence, the ellipsis.
8. Sylvie Lindeperg, for whose assistance I am very grateful, informed me that this photo was found in the archives of the Contemporary Jewish Documentation Center (CDJC) (shelf number CDLX-96) during the preparations for *Night and Fog* and that, in the film's montage documentation, it was captioned as follows: "Four naked women appear in the first frame. SS in the distance. FF [fixed frame]. German photos taken in the USSR."
9. Left aside here are subsequent critiques of this film, such as those developed on the basis of knowledge acquired and reflections written in the intervening time.
10. See Lindeperg, *"Nuit et brouillard,"* 216. Adolf Eichmann (b. 1906) was sentenced to death for his role in the deportation and extermination of Jews during the war and executed in Jerusalem on 31 May 1962. See also Hannah Arendt, *Eichmann in Jerusalem* (New York: Penguin, 2006), 25: "The indictment implied not only that he had acted on purpose, which he did not deny, but out of base motives

and in the full knowledge of the criminal nature of his deeds. As for the base motives, he was perfectly sure that he was not what he called an *innerer Schweinehund*, a dirty bastard in the depths of his heart; and as for his conscience, he remembered perfectly well that he would have had a bad conscience only if he had not done what he had been ordered to do—to ship millions of men, women, and children to their death with great zeal and the most meticulous care."

11. Translator into Hebrew of a number of French poets (Baudelaire, Rimbaud, Apollinaire . . .), himself a poet, novelist, and filmmaker, Haïm Gouri (born in 1923 in Tel Aviv, where he died in 2018) attended the trial and in 1963 published his work on it, later translated into English as *Facing the Glass Booth: The Jerusalem Trial of Adolf Eichmann* (Detroit: Wayne State University Press, 2004).

12. The Fritz Bauer Institute in Frankfurt maintains the database "Cinematography of the Holocaust," which gives the timed frame-by-frame breakdown of these documentaries by Leo Hurwitz and makes it possible to identify the numerous sequences excerpted from *Nuit et brouillard*. See http://www.cine-holocaust.de. The institute is named after German judge Fritz Bauer (1903–68), who was instrumental in the hunt for Eichmann and who also played a crucial role in initiating the Frankfurt Auschwitz Trials (1963–68), where former SS officers, some of whom were Gestapo, and camp kapos were put on trial.

13. Lothar Baier, *Un Allemand né de la dernière guerre. Essai à l'usage des Français*, afterword by Nadine Fresco (Brussels: Editions Complexe, 1986), 36.

14. "Die Vergangenheit mahnt. Eine Austellung über die Geschichte der Juden und ihre Verfolgung im Dritten Reich." After its opening in West Berlin, the exhibit then traveled to Frankfurt, Hamburg, Mannheim, and Essen from spring 1960 through fall 1962.

15. Gerhard Schoenberner (1931–2012) was the first director of the House of the Wannsee Conference in Berlin, founded in 1992. In the course of a correspondence with me, he very generously sent an abundant amount of detailed information along with highly valuable explanations. His reference to "a real discovery" was made in a letter dated 16 March 2008.

16. Central Archives of the Federal Security Service of the Russian Federation (CA FSB Russia), Collection 28, inv. 7363, vol. 2. The former name of this archive, where Schoenberner discovered these photographs in 1959, had a distinctly Soviet ring to it: Central State Archive of the October Revolution (TsGAOR).

17. Gerhard Schoenberner, *Der gelbe Stern. Die Judenverfolgung in Europa, 1933 bis 1945* (Hamburg: Argument Verlag, 2013). Unlike researchers facing today's strict practices regarding copyright and the problems these cause, Schoenberner did not have to pay anything

to get copies. Neither when he asked for, and very easily obtained, a copy of these photos from the Moscow archives, nor when he published them in this book, where they, like all the others, are included only under "*Bildquellen*" (photo sources). It is also true that, in the middle of the Cold War, the Soviet Union had every reason to encourage the dissemination of documents showing the crimes that the Nazis had committed.

18. G. Schoenberner, *Der gelbe Stern*, 96–97.
19. This line of verse—"*Deutschland, du sollst die Ermodeten nicht und nicht die Mörder vergessen!*"—is taken from a passionate antiwar poem by poet, novelist, and playwright Klabund, the pseudonym of Alfred Henschke (1890–1928). This poem, "Ballade des Vergessens" ("Ballad of Forgetting"), first appeared in the collection *Die Harfenjule. Neue Zeit-, Streit- und Leidgeschichte* (Berlin: Die Schmiede, 1927), 33–36.
20. The poem "*O Deutschland bleiche Mutter*" is reproduced in, among other publications, Bertold Brecht, *Die Gedichte*, ed. Jan Knopf (Frankfurt: Suhrkamp Editions, 2007), 256–57. *Deutschland bleiche Mutter* was the title given to a 1980 film by the German director Helma Sanders-Brahms (1940–2014) in which she reconstructed life in Germany around the Second World War. Among translations of Gerhard Schoenberner's book: *L'Étoile jaune. Le génocide juif en Europe, 1933–1945* (Paris: Presses de la Cité, 1982); *The Yellow Star: The Persecution of the Jews in Europe, 1933–1945* (New York: Fordham University Press, 2004).
21. Born in Berlin in 1892, Franz Schoenberner was, from 1929 until March 1933, the last editor-in-chief of the satirical German weekly magazine *Simplicissimus*. The *Gleichschaltung* (literally, coordination), that is the term in Nazi rhetoric designating the bringing into line of all components of political, administrative, and cultural life in Germany, began in that month. In his autobiography (see below), Franz Schoenberner later alluded to "*das Bild von den moralischen Selbstmord*" (the image of moral suicide) of *Simplicissimus*, where, as in many other places and institutions in Germany, the *Gleichschaltung* was implemented immediately on its own initiative, in mid-March 1933, without having to be imposed from outside, at the time when he himself was leaving Germany on foot for Switzerland. Having brought itself into line in this way, *Simplicissimus* continued to be published until 1944. As a refugee on the French Riviera, Franz Schoenberner was among the first German and Austrian opponents exiled in Southern France to be detained as "nationals of hostile powers" at the Camp des Milles, opened near Aix-en-Provence in September 1939. After having immigrated to the United States in 1941, he wrote an autobiography: *Confessions of a European Intellectual* (New York: Macmillan, 1946). The reference to *Simplicissimus*'s

"suicide" was taken from the memoir's German translation, *Bekenntnisse eines europäischen Intellektuellen* (Munich: Kreisselmeier Verlag, 1964), 343. Franz Schoenberner died near New York in 1970. The essentially complete collection of *Simplicissimus* (1896–1944), a color-illustrated weekly magazine to which a number of talented cartoonists and caricaturists contributed, is available at www.simplicissimus.com. Hans Zimmermann, the site's webmaster, kindly informed me of the reference to the magazine's "moral suicide."

22. See Philippe Ben, *Le Monde*, 4 April 1961: "And yet I know of few books of this kind that may be compared to that of Mr. Schoenberner. And not only because of its perfect description of the mind-boggling atmosphere in which both victims and perpetrators lived. What makes Mr. Schoenberner's book exceptional is above all the clarity of its exposition, the subdued tone of its narrator, who continually supports his statements with official texts. . . . Do the German people, especially the German youth, read this book? That's the essential question."

23. G. Schoenberner, *Der gelbe Stern*, 7.

24. Nadine Fresco and Martine Leibovici, "Une vie à l'oeuvre," foreword to Anne-Lise Stern, *Le Savoir-déporté. Camps, histoire, psychanalyse* (Paris: Éditions du Seuil, 2004; repr. series *Points-Essais*, 2007), 12.

25. See Lindeperg, "*Nuit et brouillard*," 181.

26. See Lindeperg, "*Nuit et brouillard*," chapter 12: "L'exil de la langue: Paul Celan traducteur," 181–90.

27. "Erreichbar, nah und unverloren blieb inmitten der Verluste dies eine: die Sprache./Sie, die Sprache, blieb unverloren, ja, trozt allem. Aber sie mußte nun hindurchgehen durch ihre eigenen Antwortlosigkeiten, hindurchgehen durch furchtbares Verstummen, hindurchgehen durch die tausend Finsternisse todbringender Rede. Sie ging hindurch und gab keine Worte her für das, was geschah; aber sie ging durch diese Geschehen. Ging hindurch und durfte wieder zutage treten, 'angereichert' von all dem." Paul Celan, "Speech on the Occasion of Receiving the Literature Prize of the Free Hanseatic City of Bremen [26 January 1958]," in *Selected Poems and Prose of Paul Celan*, trans. John Felstiner (New York: W. W. Norton, 2001), 395. Born in 1920 in Czernowitz, in what was then Romania (today Ukraine), of Jewish parents, both of whom were deported, Paul Antschel lived in Paris beginning in 1948. The name Celan, under which his poems and other writings appeared, is an anagram of the Romanian written form of his name, Ancel. He committed suicide in the spring of 1970 in Paris by throwing himself into the Seine. His life, his intellectual work, and his psychological suffering are apparent in the correspondence he engaged in with his wife, Gisèle Celan-Lestrange, and with a childhood friend, Ilana Shmueli, with whom he had an affair some months before his suicide. See Paul

Celan and Gisèle Celan-Lestrange, *Correspondance (1951–1970)*, with a selection of letters from Paul Celan to his son Éric, ed. and annotated by Bernard Badiou, with the support of Éric Celan, vol. 1: *Lettres*, vol. 2: *Commentaires et illustrations* (Paris: Éditions du Seuil, series *La Librairie du XXIe siècle*, 2001); Paul Celan and Ilana Shmueli, *Correspondance (1965–1970)*, ed. Ilana Shmueli and Thomas Sparr, trans. and ed. Bertrand Badiou (Paris: Éditions du Seuil, series *La Librairie du XXIe siècle*, 2006).

28. The site http://eislermusic.com (no longer available, possibly due to copyright disputes) contained many audio excerpts from Eisler's oeuvre: chamber music, compositions for Brecht's poems, for the RKO Hollywood films, etc. For example, one could listen to the Berlin actor Ernst Busch sing a Tucholsky text Eisler set to music, or retrieve the lyrics to the song "Eisler on the Go," which American folk singer Woodie Guthrie (1912–67) wrote when Eisler was forced to leave the United States in 1948. Eisler was part of a group of artists accused by the House Committee on Un-American Activities of being a Communist or sympathetic to the Communist party, and therefore boycotted by Hollywood studios. One of the members of this Committee, a certain Richard Nixon, had confirmed that Hanns Eisler was "perhaps the most important to appear before this committee." Not only with Brecht, but Eisler also became reacquainted with Arnold Schoenberg in California. A great many German and Austrian artists and writers were living in California at the time, under varying material and psychological conditions, whom the Nazi regime had forced into exile and whose books it burned: Thomas Mann, Heinrich Mann, Ludwig Marcuse, Erich Maria Remarque, Lion Feuchtwanger, Alfred Döblin, Franz Werfel and Alma Mahler, Bruno Walter . . .
29. Lindeperg, *"Nuit et brouillard,"* 133.
30. Michel Bouquet in a radio interview. Cited in Lindeperg, *"Nuit et brouillard,"* 129.
31. "June 29—I am writing about the Russian epidemic of Judeophobia of the year 1891 in the Germany of 1932 that was achieved through an even more pernicious epidemic" (in Simon Doubnov, *Le Livre de ma vie. Souvenirs et réflexions. Matériaux pour l'histoire de mon temps*, trans. from Russian and annotated by Brigitte Bernheimer, preface by Henri Minczeles (Paris: Éditions du Cerf, 2001), 1,092.
32. *Der Stürmer* (The Stormer), founded in 1923 and edited by Julius Streicher, was characterized by a profusion of heavily antisemitic caricatures. This weekly was published right up until 1945, and had reached a subscription of 400,000 copies ten years before that. At Nuremberg in 1946, Streicher was one of the twelve sentenced to death among the twenty-four accused at the trial of the main Nazi leaders. The definition of the *Stürmer* as a "news outlet

for antisemitic hate" is from Victor Klemperer, *The Language of the Third Reich: LTI. Lingua Tertii Imperii*, trans. Martin Brady (London: Bloomsbury, 2000), 291.

33. Klemperer, *The Language of the Third Reich*, 11–12. The son of a rabbi and a convert to Protestantism, the German philologist Victor Klemperer (1881–1960) taught at the University of Dresden until he was forced to retire in 1935. *LTI*, Klemperer's analysis of the language established by the regime, was first published in East Germany in 1947. It is based on entries from the diary that Klemperer kept in Dresden during the twelve years of Nazism. He dubbed that language LTI, *Lingua Tertii Imperii*, the language of the Third Reich. Klemperer's journals were translated into English by Martin Chalmers and appeared under the titles *I Shall Bear Witness: The Diaries of Victor Klemperer (1933–1941)*; *To the Bitter End: The Diaries of Victor Klemperer (1942–1945)*; and *The Lesser Evil: The Diaries of Victor Klemperer (1945–1959)*, all published by Weidenfeld and Nicolson (1998, 1999, 2003).

34. Klemperer, *Geschichte der französischen Literatur im 18. Jahrhundert* (Tübingen: Max Niemeyer Verlag, 1954).

35. Klemperer, *The Language of the Third Reich*, 11–12.

36. Three days later, the *Jüdische Rundschau*, the bi-weekly Zionist newspaper in Berlin, printed an editorial by then-editor Robert Weltsch (Prague, 1891; Jerusalem, 1982) with the title "Tragt ihn mit Stoltz, den gelben Fleck!" (Wear it with pride, the yellow stain!) in large letters. The clear warning Weltsch addresses to his German co-religionists stands in sharp contrast to the conviction held by so many of them at that time—those who believed, or were inclined to believe, that because they had been present for a thousand years in Germany, as they were fond of saying, they did not have to fear the Nazi regime. Weltsch wrote: "We live in a new era. The national revolution of the German people is the signal, visible from afar, that the old world of ideas [*die alte Begriffswelt*] has collapsed. This will doubtless be painful for many, but, in such a world, only the one who looks reality in the face will assert himself [*sich behaupten*]. . . . Jews, seize David's shield and wear it with pride!" (*Jüdische Rundschau*, 4 April 1933). All issues of this newspaper (which appeared from 1902 to 1938), as well as those of more than one hundred other Jewish periodicals published in German between 1806 and 1938, are available on the site www.compactmemory.de.

37. *Völkischer Beobachter*, 2–3 April 1933. The 29 March issue was devoted to specific uses of propaganda for organizing and prolonging the boycott.

38. Recall the title of Raul Hilberg's book: *Perpetrators, Victims, Bystanders: The Jewish Catastrophe 1933–1945* (New York: Harper Perennial, 1993).

39. "Aufkleber fur jüdische Geschäfte im Jahre 1933," Bildarchiv Preussischer Kulturbesitz, Berlin, cited in Sybil Milton, "The Camera as Weapon: Documentary Photography and the Holocaust," *Holocaust and Genocide Studies* 1, no. 1 (1986): 27–61. In another article from the same period, Milton writes: "Although there are more than two million photographs held in the public archives of more than twenty countries, the images reproduced in the scholarly and popular literature for the last forty years are, in terms of their quality as well as the ground they cover and their content, very repetitive and in large part taken from Gerhard Schoenberner's classic work *The Yellow Star*, which appeared in 1960" (Milton, "Photography as Evidence of the Holocaust," *History of Photography* 23, vol. 4 [1999]: 303–12).
40. See in particular Walter Laqueur's book *The Terrible Secret: Suppression of the Truth about Hitler's Final Solution* (Boston: Little, Brown and Company, 1980). And that by David S. Wyman, *The Abandonment of the Jews: America and the Holocaust, 1941–1945* (New York: Pantheon Books, 1984).
41. "What can be said of the German population at large in the 1930s? Was the bulk of the German population swept along by the Nazis' antisemitic tide? Only in part, according to the detailed research of historians like Ian Kershaw, Otto Dov Kulka, and David Bankier, who have reached a surprising degree of consensus on this issue. For the 1933–1939 period, these three historians distinguish between a minority of party activists, for whom antisemitism was an urgent priority, and the bulk of the German population, for whom it was not. . . . Most important, however, a gulf had opened up between the Jewish minority and the general population. The latter, while not mobilized around strident and violent antisemitism, were increasingly 'apathetic,' 'passive,' and 'indifferent' to the fate of the former." These lines are taken from the afterword to the paperback edition of Christopher R. Browning, *Ordinary Men: Reserve Police Battalion 101 and the Final Solution in Poland* (New York: Harper Perennial, 1998), 199–200.
42. G. Schoenberner, *Der gelbe Stern*, 7.
43. Primo Levi, *The Drowned and the Saved*, trans. Raymond Rosenthal (New York: Random House, 1988), 203.
44. Thomas Mann, *Order of the Day: Political Essays and Speeches of Two Decades* (New York: Alfred A. Knopf, 1942), 155.
45. Martine Leibovici, "Les fables politiques de Charlotte Beradt," introduction to the French translation of Charlotte Beradt, *Rêver sous le IIIe Reich*, trans. Pierre Saint-Germain, afterwords by Reinhart Koselleck and François Gantheret (Paris: Payot, 2002), 23.
46. *Vor aller Augen* is the title of an important book: Klaus Hesse and Philipp Springer, *Vor aller Augen: Fotodokumente des nationalso-*

zialistischen Terrors in der Provinz, ed. Reinhard Rürup (Essen: Klartext Verlag, 2002). This book is a catalogue accompanying an exhibition the authors conceived for the Stiftung Topographie des Terrors (Topography of Terror Documentation Center) in Berlin (www.topographie.de/en/topography-of-terror). The exhibit was on display in Berlin in 2002–2003 before then traveling to other German cities. The photographs reproduced here pp. 13, 17, 29, 31 are printed on pp. 100, 145, and 153 of *Vor aller Augen*. Many images of the Nazi terror of course exist in several other publications and internet sites. But what makes *Vor aller Augen* an important book is that the hundreds of photographs it contains and their detailed captions powerfully show how, until deportation, each of the successive steps of this terror took place before everyone's eyes.

47. "SA and SS, the *Schutzstaffel* . . . or praetorian guard, are abbreviations which became so satisfied with themselves that they were no longer really abbreviations at all; they took on independent meanings which entirely obscured their original signification" (Klemperer, *The Language of the Third Reich*, 63).

48. Hesse and Springer, *Vor aller Augen*, 130–33.

49. Photographs of the punitive, eroticized violence done to shaven women in France at the end of the war, amid the sneering of surrounding faces, have perhaps remained all the more imprescriptible into memory because of their similarity to the very same barbarity practiced by an occupier from whom France had finally been liberated.

50. Jean Améry, *At the Mind's Limits: Contemplations by a Survivor on Auschwitz and Its Realities*, trans. Sidney Rosenfeld and Stella P. Rosenfeld (Bloomington: Indiana University Press, 1980), 85–86.

51. Paul Niedermann (who died in 2018) was born in 1927 in Karlsruhe and was deported from there with his entire family on 22 October 1940. These accounts are excerpts from an interview I conducted with him on 31 May 2002 at the Maison d'Izieu (see https://www.memorializieu.eu) as part of days that were devoted to filming the testimonials of several people who had found refuge there as children during the war.

52. Hesse and Springer, *Vor aller Augen*, 105 (for Münster), 92–93 (Ober-Ramstadt), 116 (Edenkoben), and 100 (Mosbach).

53. Describing the vandalism of the Munich synagogues in his journal, Joseph Goebbels explains: "We extinguish only insofar as is necessary for the neighbouring buildings. Otherwise, everything must burn" (cited in Saul Friedländer, *Nazi Germany and the Jews*, vol. 1: *The Years of Persecution 1933–1939* [New York: Harper Perennial, 1998], 272).

54. On the eruption and repercussions of "Kristallnacht," see Raul Hilberg, *The Destruction of the European Jews*, 3rd ed. (New Haven: Yale University Press, 2003), 1:40, 42.
55. Niedermann interview, 2002.
56. "[Himmler] ordered his forces into action to prevent large-scale looting and, incidentally, to fill his concentration camps with 20,000 Jews." Note at the bottom of the page: "On November 11, 1938, Security Police chief Heydrich reported approximately 20,000 arrests to Göring. PS-3058. The final number, however, was greater. From Austria and southern Germany, 10,911 were delivered to Dachau. . . . Several hundred died in the three camps [Dachau, Buchenwald, Sachsenhausen]. All but a few were released within a few months" (Hilberg, *The Destruction of the European Jews*, 1:38).
57. See Saul Friedländer, *Nazi Germany and the Jews*, vol. 2: *The Years of Extermination 1939–1945* (New York: HarperCollins, 2007), where the author cites from a diary kept by a Jew from Breslau: "January 30, 1940: Jews need travel permits; March 27, 1940: Barber service is only available until nine o'clock in the morning . . . ; June 20, 1940: Jews are forbidden to sit on all public benches; . . . ; July 29, 1940: No fruit available for Jews" (p. 96).
58. The figure of 6,540 people is the one given by Gerhard J. Teschner, on the basis of numerous sources and earlier studies, in *Die Deportation der badischen und saarpfälzischen Juden am 22. Oktober 1940* (Frankfurt: Peter Lang Verlag, 2002), 107.
59. These remarks are reproduced in Dr. Joseph Weill, *Contribution à l'histoire des camps d'internement dans l'Anti-France* (Paris: CDJC, Éd. du Centre, 1946), 23.
60. Niedermann interview, 2002.
61. The Nazi leadership attempted to make the idea of a Jewish settlement in Madagascar (an idea already in existence before the war) a reality in the spring of 1940. The idea was to have the SS manage this "ghetto island" to which European Jews would be sent at a rate of a million per year. But no sooner had "the alluring vision of a quick and total solution to the Jewish question cast its magic spell" than the Nazis abandoned the plan at the end of 1940. See Christopher R. Browning, with contributions by Jürgen Matthäus, *The Origins of the Final Solution: The Evolution of Nazi Jewish Policy, September 1939–March 1942* (Lincoln: University of Nebraska Press, 2004); see chapter "The Madagascar Plan," 88 and 89).
62. The number of arrests by city and by administrative district (*Landkreis*) of these German Jews on 22 October 1940 are available at https://de.wikipedia.org/wiki/Wagner-Bürckel-Aktion, an *Aktion* so named because Robert Wagner, the Gauleiter (the head of a *Gau*, a region) of Baden, and Joseph Bürckel, the Gauleiter of Saarpfalz-Kreis,

were the ones who organized these arrests. The series of Lörrach photographs described here are in *Vor aller Augen* on pages 142–47.
63. "The mortality rate of inmates aged 60–64 years in the Gurs Camp is twelve times higher than the national average for the same age range on the eve of the War, and for the age-group of 70–74 years, it is nearly sixteen times larger. The old age of those from Baden who perished in the camp, although part of the explanation, is not a decisive factor. The state of the Bearnese facility, the lack of hygiene, the inadequacy of the food, the darkness and chill of the barracks, the idleness imposed by circumstances and the grief at having lost everything struck the fatal blow to beings already weakened by old age." Claude Laharie, *Le camp de Gurs, 1939–1945. Un aspect méconnu de l'histoire de Vichy*, preface by Artur London (Pau: J&D Éditions, 1993), 195.
64. Among those expelled from Baden were four children from Mannheim, aged two, four, eight, and eleven. Given how overcrowded the Gurs Internment Camp had become by the spring of 1941, a large number of those interned, including two of these children, were transferred to Rivesaltes Camp. Via the networks of the OSE (*Oeuvre de Secours aux Enfants*), all four of them arrived at the village of Izieu in the early summer of 1943, from which they were deported the following spring. The parents of these four children had already died in the interim, gassed at Auschwitz.
65. In 1936, this Nazi formulation—"without the solution to the Jewish question, no final solution for the German people"—still oscillated between *Lösung* (solution to a problem, or chemical solution) and *Endlösung* (final solution). By 1942, there would be no more oscillation: the solution was thenceforth *die Endlösung der Judenfrage*, the Final Solution to the Jewish question. When Lörrach's mayor gave a speech in the year 2000 at the commemoration of the sixtieth anniversary of the deportation of the city's Jews, she recalled this sentence, which Streicher, together with Robert Wagner, had written in the city's guestbook.
66. Niedermann interview, 2002.
67. Philippe Burrin, *La France à l'heure allemande. 1940–1944* (Paris: Éditions du Seuil, 1995), 73. See also Chapter 7: "Montoire," 105–19.
68. Montoire seems no closer than Vichy to getting rid of its name's association with the French–German collaboration of the Occupation years. In a flyer entitled "The Historic Train Station of Montoire-sur-le-Loir (http://www.mairie-montoire.fr/dyn/tourisme_culture_patrimoine/depliant-2017.pdf), available on the website of its small museum, one can read (in French and English): "Montoire entered the history books on the 22nd and 24th October 1940 when Laval met with Hitler, followed two days later by the famous meeting between Pétain and the Chancellor of the Reich. The 'handshake' started

four long years of collaboration between Nazi Germany and Vichy France."

69. These comments were made before the German Armistice Commission at Wiesbaden by General Paul Doyen, who directed the French delegation from September 1940 to July 1941. See the *Documents français de la commission d'armistice*, 4:98, cited by Éric Alary, "Les juifs et la ligne de démarcation. 1940–1943," *Les Cahiers de la Shoah* 5, no. 1 (2001): 45n11.

70. See Laharie, *Le Camp de Gurs*, 57–58. Three months later, on 10 January 1941, a new bulletin taught prefects how to master the updated Vichy language: "The structures at Le Vernet and at Rieucros must be called concentration camps, the foreigners there are detainees. Gurs, Argelès (and all new structures to be created in the future) must be called 'hosting centers.'" (Cited in Anne Boitel, *Le Camp de Rivesaltes 1941–1942. Du centre d'hébergement au "Drancy de la zone libre*," preface by Michel Cadé, afterword by Serge Klarsfeld [Perpignan: Presses Universitaires de Perpignan, 2001], 23.) Klarsfeld was the one who described Rivesaltes as "Drancy de la zone libre" (The Drancy of the Free Zone).

71. This excerpt from a *"Note pour le ministre"* dated 25 October 1940, issued by the political directorate of the Ministry of Foreign Affairs, is cited in Anne Grynberg, *Les Camps de la honte. Les internés juifs des camps français, 1939–1944* (Paris: La Découverte, 1999), 142–43.

72. The comment about the Vichy and the German officials is made by Michael R. Marrus and Robert O. Paxton in *Vichy France and the Jews* (Stanford: Stanford University Press, 1995), 12, where they also cite this 1941 compendium.

73. "Complicit even before having understood the inevitable extent of their own compromise, Vichy officials, in this regard, as in all others, headed further and further down the road of crimes against the permanent values of civilization and against humanity" (Weill, *Contribution à l'histoire des camps d'internement*, 10).

74. Article 1 of the first German ordinance, dated 27 September 1940, which imposed the registration of Jews in the Occupied Zone, declared that "a Jew is one who belongs to or used to belong to the Jewish religion, or who has more than two Jewish grandparents." Article 1 of the French law dated 3 October 1940, the "Law pertaining to the status of Jews," declared that "for the purposes of the present law, a Jew is one who has three grandparents of the Jewish race; or who has two grandparents of that race, if his or her spouse is Jewish." This German ordinance and this French law are included in, among other books, a calendar: Serge Klarsfeld, *Le Calendrier de la persécution des juifs en France, 1940–1944* (Paris: FFDJF & The Beate Klarsfeld Foundation, 1993), 23, 25. Not all occupied countries were as zealous as France. Fifteen months later, the attendees of the "Conference

on the Final Solution of the Jewish Question" held at Wannsee in 1942, after having determined the number of Jews still alive in occupied countries, noted that this *Judenzahl* (Jew count) only covered *Glaubensjuden* (Jews of faith); a full registration of Jews according to racial criteria was still lacking. Regarding France itself, the language of the protocol was rather serene: "In occupied and unoccupied France, the registration of Jews for evacuation [*zur Evakuierung*] will in all probability proceed without great difficulty [*ohne große Schwierigkeiten*]." The complete (fifteen-page) typed text of the Wannsee Conference protocol is available on the website of the House of the Wannsee Conference: https://www.ghwk.de/fileadmin/Redaktion/PDF/Konferenz/protokoll-januar1942_barrierefrei.pdf. The name given to this memorial and educational site, inaugurated in 1992, comes from the fact that fifty years earlier, on 20 January 1942, this Wannsee villa near Berlin, purchased by the SS in 1940, was where Reinhard Heydrich, the chief of the RSHA (the Reich Security Main Office), assembled fourteen officials from the SS, the police, and the Nazi Party for this "*Besprechung über die Endlösung der Judenfrage*" (discussion about the final solution of the Jewish question), according to the precise terms used in the protocol of this meeting.

75. This telegram sent on 18 October 1940 by Jacques Guérard, the Chief of Staff of the Minister of Foreign Affairs, to the Ambassador of France in Washington, is reproduced in Klarsfeld, *Le Calendrier de la persécution des juifs en France*, 30–31. Jacques Guérard, who from April 1942 to the end of the Occupation served as Secretary-General to Pierre Laval, whose "damned soul" he was (Henry Rousso, *Pétain et la fin de la collaboration. Sigmaringen 1944–1945* [Brussels: Complexe, 1984], 40), took refuge in Spain at the end of the war, after which he was sentenced to death in absentia in 1947. He returned to France in 1955 and was given a suspended prison sentence of five years by the High Court of Justice in 1958.

76. Born in 1904 to a Jewish father and a non-Jewish mother, the left radical–socialist and freemason Jean Zay entered politics by participating in the campaign of the 1924 legislative elections in the city of Orléans. This got him called out in the local Communist newspaper, *Le Travailleur du Loiret*, as "this young man with the face of a *métèque*" and "this hateful one-track mind that lies in your denaturalized Jewish skull." Throughout the 1930s, the far-right came after this man, who was as "enraged and shameless as so many of his race" and who "exposes himself as the eternal wanderer, an International in the worst sense of the word" ("La voix juive," *Le Journal du Loiret*, 16 February 1934). The "language used by Mr. Jean Zay about the French flag," condemned in 1940 by the Chief of Staff of the Minister of Foreign Affairs, involved a one-page antimilitarist literary pastiche, "Le Drapeau" (The Flag), written by Zay when he was

nineteen and never published. The far-right later took the trouble of publishing it to feed its incessant antisemitic condemnations of this "International." Made Minister of National Education in the Popular Front government in May 1936, and reappointed to this office until the war, Jean Zay was arrested on 15 August 1940, on the order of the Vichy government. Tried at Clermont-Ferrand by a military court, the very same day (4 October 1940) of the signing of the "law pertaining to foreign nationals of Jewish race," in a parody of a trial that lasted only this one day, sentenced to deportation and to dishonorable discharge from the military, he was imprisoned at Riom, a small town in the center of France. In 1942, it was collaborator Philippe Henriot's turn to condemn "this little Jew who found himself thrust into politics by the aberration of universal suffrage" and who "started off in life by attempting to soil the flag of the country that hosted him" (Philippe Henriot, foreword to the *Carnets secrets de Jean Zay* [Paris: Les Éditions de France, 1942], i–iii). All quotations here are taken from Olivier Loubes's article "D'un drapeau l'autre. Jean Zay (1914–1940)," *Vingtième Siècle. Revue d'histoire* 71 (2001): 37–51. On 20 June 1944, provided with a transfer order signed by André Baillet, the Commissioner of Prisons, some men from the militia pulled Jean Zay from his cell and assassinated him in a forest. His body, which had been thrown down a well, was discovered in 1946 but only identified two years later, after the arrest of one of his assassins. I am much obliged to Hélène Mouchard-Zay, the founder (in 1991) and president of the Cercil (Centre d'étude et de recherche sur les camps d'internement du Loiret), for the information she provided me about Jean Zay, her father.

77. "The very essence of marriage, such as it is instituted in our morals, is to unite a young virginal woman to a fully-grown man, and to submit the education of the virgin to the experience of the man. At the basis of the system is found the principle, or, in my opinion, the prejudice of the virginity of the girls. But, in agreeing that the girls must reach marriage in this state of naivety and ignorance, still it would be necessary that these novices have good masters, and that their conjugal preparation be placed in good hands. The current system prevents girls from acquiring an even theoretical experience of love before marriage. . . . As soon as we have the power to do so, we have the right to transform procreation into a voluntary and reflected act, and it is extraordinary that, over so many centuries, thinking creatures are able to link to the expression of an instinct the most serious act that is given them to accomplish. Perhaps these ideas, and the results they would bring, are still too new for our society" (Léon Blum, *Du mariage* [Paris: Paul Ollendorff, 1907], 87, 314–15). At the time of its publication, this book's innovative freedom, in content and in tone, earned its author criticism both from the left and the

right. But it was mostly the far right, particularly during the Popular Front government, which, amid its incessant attacks on Blum, denounced the analyses and propositions of this regularly republished book (the 1947 edition, for instance, was the 152nd).

78. "Oedipus, meanwhile, is hounded from Thebes. Guided by his daughter Antigone, he lives out his life near Colonus, a *deme*, or hamlet, outside Athens. . . . And now here he is in the last days of his wanderings, without a place, without attachment, without roots—a migrant. Theseus extends him hospitality; he does not make Oedipus a citizen of Athens, but he does accord him the status of *metooikoss*, or resident alien—a privileged foreigner. He will live in this land that is not his own and settle here. . . . Oedipus becomes an official alien in Athens" (Jean-Pierre Vernant, *The Universe, the Gods, and Men*, trans. Lisa Asher [New York: Harper Perennial, 2002], 170–71).
79. Gérard Noiriel, *Immigration, antisémitisme et racisme en France (XIXe–XXe siècle). Discours publics, humiliations privées* (Paris: Fayard, 2007), 460.
80. Bulletin dated 14 April 1938 from Albert Sarraut, Minister of the Interior. Cited in Grynberg, *Les Camps de la honte*, 32.
81. This decree-law, dated 14 May 1938, restricted the allocation of identity cards. The report presenting it specifies that the State may "consider a scale in liberties granted to workers for practicing their professional activity on our soil. Should these liberties be reduced to a minimum, the identity card would be valid only for the profession and the department for which they were issued" (cited in Noiriel, *Immigration, antisémitisme et racisme en France*, 461).
82. The complete text of these decree-laws dated 2 May and 12 November 1938, and especially of the reports preceding them, can be found at "Vichy avant Vichy" on the website http://pages.livresdeguerre.net/pages/sujet.php?id=docddp&su=103.
83. Robert Brasillach, "Nous, nous continuons" ("As for us, we continue"), *Je suis partout*, 2 June 1941. Cited in Michel Laval, *Brasillach ou la trahison du clerc* (Paris: Hachette, 1992), 116.
84. Weill, *Contribution à l'histoire des camps d'internement*, 180.
85. The story of Leopold, Anna, Kurt, and Elisabeth Feiertag is recounted in *Pithiviers-Auschwitz. 17 juillet 1942, 6h15*, a collection of testimonies compiled by Monique Novodorsqui-Deniau, with preface by Simone Weil, ed. Katy Hazan, Benoît Verny, and Nadine Fresco (Orléans: Éditions Cercil, 2006), 257–61.
86. "Faintly seen [on a photograph made in Amsterdam in 1942], the *Jood* does not appear in block letters or in any other commonly used script. The characters were specially designed for this particular purpose (and similarly drawn in the languages of the countries of deportation: *Jude, Juif, Jood*, and so on) in a crooked, repulsive, and vaguely threatening way, intended to evoke the Hebrew alphabet and

yet remain easily decipherable" (Friedländer, *The Years of Extermination*, xiv).

87. Klemperer, *The Language of the Third Reich*, 171. In 1979, negationist Robert Faurisson (1929–2018) speculated that those who were forced to wear the yellow star "were like prisoners of war on supervised parole. Hitler preoccupied himself perhaps less with the Jewish question than with ensuring the security of the German soldier. The average German trooper would have been incapable of distinguishing Jews from non-Jews. The Star of David identified them" (Robert Faurisson, interview with *Storia Illustrata* no. 261, [Aug. 1979], in Serge Thion, *Vérité historique ou vérité politique? Le dossier de l'affaire Faurisson. La question des chambres à gaz* [Paris: La Vieille Taupe, 1980], 172).

88. Gertrude Schneider, who was herself deported with her family in February 1942 from Vienna to Riga at the age of thirteen, has written about the deportation of German and Austrian Jews to Latvia in *Muted Voices: Jewish Survivors of Latvia Remember* (New York: Philosophical Library, 1987); *Journey into Terror: Story of the Riga Ghetto* (Westport, CT: Praeger, 2001); and *The Unfinished Road: Jewish Survivors of Latvia Look Back* (New York: Praeger, 1991). During my correspondence with her in 2007 and 2008, Schneider very generously had her German publisher send me a copy of her latest book, *Reise in den Tod. Deutsche Juden in Riga, 1941–1944* (Berlin: Hentrich, 2006), which contains a number of reports and letters by the Nazi administration on the subject of the operations to "evacuate" German Jews to Riga. The preface was written by historian Nobert Kampe, director of the House of the Wannsee Conference. Listed last (a matter of hierarchy) on the list of the fifteen participants at this 29 January 1942 conference, SS functionary Rudolf Lange had been "Commander of Security Police and Security Service for the District General of Latvia acting as deputy of the Commander in Chief of Security Police and the SD for the Reichskommissariat Ostland" since the previous month, as was specified in the conference's protocol. Lange was one of those involved in the deportation of German Jews to Riga. According to the website of the House of the Wannsee Conference, he committed suicide in February 1945 in Poznan. According to Raul Hilberg (*The Destruction of the European Jews*, 3:1,184), he is "believed killed in the Battle of Poznań, 1945."

89. Since 1947, more than 350,000 photographs and 1,000 films taken during the war by members of the Propaganda Kompanien have been kept in the archives of the French Ministry of Defense at the Fort d'Ivry, in the suburbs of Paris.

90. "Propagandaweisung des Reichspropagandaministers für den 2.10. 1939," cited in Daniel Uziel, "Wehrmacht Propaganda Troops and the Jews," trans. William Templer, *Yad Vashem Studies* 29 (2001): 33.

91. *Propaganda Kompanie: Deutsche Soldaten beim Fotografieren einer Hinrichtung, Russland 1941/42*, Bundesarchiv Bild 101/287/872/28a. This photograph is reproduced in an article in which the author speculates that such shots—"Trophäen in Brieftaschen" (trophies in wallets), found on killed or captured soldiers—might have served as *Angstabwehr* (defenses against fear). Perhaps the depiction of slaughtered enemies would have served the soldiers as an amulet against the risk of their own deaths. See Kathrin Hoffmann-Curtius, "Trophäen in Brieftaschen: Fotografien von Wehrmachts-, SS- und Polizei-Verbrechen," Kunsttexte.de, March 2002, available at https://docplayer.org/17128503-Trophaeen-in-brieftaschen-fotografien-von-wehrmachts-ss-und-polizei-verbrechen.html. See also Bernd Hüppauf, "Emptying the Gaze: Framing Violence through the Viewfinder," in *War of Extermination: The German Military in World War II, 1941–1944*, ed. Hannes Heer and Klaus Neumann (New York: Berghahn Books, 2000), 345–77.
92. Uziel, "Wehrmacht Propaganda Troops and the Jews," 27–65. The article "Juden unter sich" (Jews among themselves) was published in the *Berliner Illustrierte Zeitung*, 24 July 1941.
93. During the Occupation, business continued as usual. What applies to the soldiers of the Wehrmacht also applies to the civilians of the occupied countries. The French edition of the Nazi propaganda magazine *Signal*, which was sustained by written and photographic content from the Propaganda Kompanien, contains the following advertisement for the Zeiss Ikon company: "Haven't you forgotten something? Quick! Examine the contents of your pocket or your handbag: the wallet, the keys, the identity card, everything's there; yes, but maybe something almost as important is still missing: the handheld camera Tenax. Small and light, this small-format camera—24 x 24 mm—instantly ready for use, fits in any pocket. That's why it should always be with you, so that you can enjoy the many scenes that present themselves before your eyes every day ..." *Signal* was "the high-status organ of the German army, with more than 2.5 million copies distributed in various editions, including one in French and one in Arabic, destined for North Africa" (Pascal Ory, interview in *Beaux-Arts* 288 [June 2008]: 107). An exhibition entitled "Les Parisiens sous l'Occupation: Photographies en couleurs d'André Zucca" (The Parisians under the Occupation: Color Pictures by André Zucca)—devoted to a French photographer who collaborated with *Signal*—was mounted at the Bibliothèque Historique de la Ville de Paris from 25 March to 1 July 2008. Regarding the objections raised by the absence of critical contextualization in this highly colored portrayal of nonchalance and liberty, see, for example, the article by Philippe Dagen, "Des photographies de propagande nazie provoquent un malaise," *Le Monde*, 12 April 2008. Following these objections, the arti-

cle of the first word of the exhibition's title was made indefinite: "Des Parisiens sous l'Occupation" (Parisians under the Occupation").

94. The title of the book edited by Ernst Klee, Willy Dressen, and Volker Riess, *"The Good Old Days": The Holocaust as Seen by Its Perpetrators and Bystanders*, trans. Deborah Burstone, with foreword by Hugh Trevor-Roper (Old Saybrook, CT: Konecky & Konecky, 1996). Kurt Franz (1914–98) was arrested in 1959 and stood trial as one of the ten accused in Düsseldorf at the Treblinka trial (1964–65), during which this photo album was produced. Sentenced to life imprisonment, Franz was freed for health reasons in 1993.

95. In Claude Lanzmann's film *Shoah*, former SS-Unterscharführer Franz Suchomel sings this "Treblinka song" to the director, and then comments: "Do not blame me, you wanted History, I am telling you History. It was Franz who wrote the words. The melody came from Buchenwald, from the concentration camp where Franz was a guard." For the text of the film, see Claude Lanzmann, *Shoah*, preface by Simone de Beauvoir (Paris: Gallimard, series *Folio*, 2001 [1985]), 154.

96. In the memoir that he wrote at the Kraków Prison where he was detained before his trial and until his execution on 16 April 1947, Rudolf Höss, Commandant of the Auschwitz-Birkenau camp for the greater part of the war, wrote about Himmler: "As Reichsführer-SS, his person was inviolable. His basic orders, issued in the name of the Führer, were sacred" (Rudolf Höss, *Commandant of Auschwitz*, trans. Constantine FitzGibbon, and introduction by Primo Levi [London: Phoenix Press, 2000], 145).

97. For more on the Einsatzgruppen, their interaction with the Wehrmacht, and, more broadly, the stages of the extermination of the Jews beginning in June 1941, see, among others, Browning, *The Origins of the Final Solution* (see above, n61).

98. Arno Mayer has written that, by "naming the eastern campaign Operation Barbarossa, Hitler indicated that he saw elective affinities between Friedrich Barbarossa (Frederick I) and himself. Barbarossa was the German Emperor who in the twelfth century, in addition to setting his sights on eastern Europe, had forced his own anointment before taking the cross to the Holy Land. For Hitler to preach a crusade against the Bolshevik regime and ideology was not to mask but to sacralize his own geopolitical designs and weapons" (Arno J. Mayer, *Why Did the Heavens Not Darken? The "Final Solution" in History* [New York: Pantheon, 1988], 34). On pages 226–31 of this book, the author recounts the massacres of Jews, particularly in Germany, carried out by participants in the 1095–96 crusade. In the prologue, he cites an excerpt from *The Chronicle of Solomon bar Simson,* written after the massacre of the Jews of Mainz: "Why did the heavens not darken and the stars not withhold their radiance, why did not the sun and moon turn dark?" (p. 26).

99. "... the invasion of the Soviet Union cost the lives of some 24 million Soviet citizens, of whom many more than half were civilians, and ravaged immense regions of western Russia, from Leningrad in the north to Stalingrad in the south. More than three million prisoners of war from the Red Army, 60 percent of the total number of Soviet soldiers taken prisoner, would die in captivity under the watch of German jailers. Although the Soviet Union seemed like a military superpower after the war, it would in fact take many decades to recover from the human tragedy and economic disaster of the German occupation" (Omer Bartov, "Guerre barbare: Politique guerrière de l'Allemagne et choix moraux pendant la Seconde Guerre mondiale," *Revue d'histoire de la Shoah* 187, *La Wehrmacht dans la Shoah* [July–Dec. 2007]: 113).
100. In *The Destruction of the European Jews*, Raul Hilberg devotes a chapter (vol. 1, chap. 7, "Mobile Killing Operations") to the organization of Einsatzgruppen A, B, C, and D by the RSHA and to the crimes they committed in the territory invaded by the Soviet Union.
101. In the final decade of the twentieth century, the Hamburg Institute for Social Research organized an exhibition named "'War of Extermination': Crimes of the Wehrmacht 1941–1944." The exhibition opened in March 1995 in Hamburg before touring to thirty-three cities in Germany and Austria. When it closed its doors in 1999, it had been seen by approximately 800,000 people. The impact of the exhibit was enormous. It stirred up a highly controversial issue because, with the aid of supporting documents, it debunked the myth of an innocent Wehrmacht. "One thinks of the hate-filled faces of 5000 Neo-Nazis in Munich or of the placards of the exhibition that had been pierced by the explosions of a bomb in Saarbrucken; remember the gibbering, furious, or powerless old men in front of the exhibition, of the moving debate in the German parliament, of the scenes of visitors in tears who recognized their fathers in the photos." This recollection was written by Hannes Heer, one of the exhibition's organizers, who recalled how it "divided the entire country." Hannes Heer, "Das Haupt der Medusa. Die Verbrechen der Wehrmacht und der Kampf um die Erinnerung in Deutschland," *Geschichte und Region/ Storia e regione* 16, no. 2 (2007): 193–94. To respond to the allegations of falsification that were brought against the exhibition's organizers, the director of the Hamburg Institute for Social Research, Jan Philipp Reemtsma, suspended it in 1999 and referred its contents to a board of historians. In its report, made public in November 2000, this board, which specified that it had examined this exhibition "with a thoroughness never before exercised for an exhibition about a subject from recent history," picked up on errors and inaccuracies in content and presentation, as well as problematic generalizations, but no falsification. This report, titled

Bericht der Kommission zur Überprüfung der Ausstellung "Vernichtungskrieg. Verbrechen der Wehrmacht, 1941–1944" is available at http://www.verbrechen-der-wehrmacht.de/pdf/bericht_kommission.pdf.

102. "Die Sonderkommandos sind berechtigt im Rahmen ihres Auftrages in eigener Verantwortung gegenüber der Zivilbevölkerung Exekutivmassnahmen zu treffen" (Regulation from 28 April 1941 regarding the action of the Sicherheitspolizei and of the Sicherheitsdienst in the Army, Bundesarchiv, Militärarchiv, RH 22/155). In a letter to Pétain on 10 November 1941, Hitler presented this operation as the result of a "last minute" decision: "If I had not decided at the last minute, on June 22, to move against the Bolshevist menace, then it could have happened only too easily that with the collapse of Germany the French Jews would have triumphed, but the French people would likewise have been plunged into a horrible catastrophe." This excerpt of the letter is cited in Friedländer, *The Years of Extermination*, 275.
103. On this issue of collaboration, see above, pp. 40–42. See also n131–34.
104. "Hinrichtung von Partisanen in Russland im Januar 1943" (Execution of Partisans in Russia in January 1943). This photograph is included in Gordon Williamson, *Die SS. Hitlers Instrument der Macht. Die Geschichte der SS, von der Schutztaffel bis zur Waffen-SS* (Munich: Kaiser Verlag, 2003), 229.
105. *Verordnungsblatt der Waffen-SS*, 2nd year, no. 11, Berlin, 15 June 1941, Militärgeschichtliches Forschungsamt, Potsdam.
106. Order by Colonel Montua of the Police Regiment Center, 11 July 1941, in Browning, *Ordinary Men*, 14.
107. "Sunday, June 22 [1941]. In two declarations, the one addressed to the nation and the other to the armies, General Antonescu announces that, taking sides with Germany, Romania is engaging in a sacred war to liberate Bessarabia and Bucovina and to annihilate Bolshevism. On his side, in a long declaration, Hitler explained the causes of the war launched against the Soviets. Before sunrise, German troops penetrated the Russian border at various points and bombarded several cities. No geographic precisions given. Molotov [the Minister of Foreign Affairs for the USSR], speaking on radio at dawn, protested against the 'aggression,' the 'brutality,' etc. Witness the Soviet wolf forced to play the role of the innocent lamb. It looks like a poor Belgian mediocrity" (Mihail Sebastian, *Journal, 1935–1944*, trans. Alain Paruit, preface by Edgar Reichmann [Paris: Stock, 2007], 327).
108. This order by General Wöhler is cited in Hilberg, *The Destruction of the European Jews*, 1:334. Otto Wohler (1894–1987) was sentenced to eight years imprisonment in October 1948 (and then freed in January 1951) by the Nuremberg Tribunal (*Case 12: The High*

Command Case) for his collaboration with Einsatzgruppe D. Ic/AO: Intelligence officer.

109. Browning, *The Origins of the Final Solution*, 265. This letter may also be found, notably in slightly modified translation, in Friedländer, *The Years of Extermination*, 214. Letters sent from the front lines by soldiers of the Wehrmacht during the Second World War have been researched in Germany and in Austria for several years now using collections preserved in a number of archives. In particular, 50,000 letters gathered in the Sterz collection of the Bibliothek für Zeitgeschichte (Library of Contemporary History) in Stuttgart. Martin Humburg studied 739 of them in *Das Gesicht des Krieges. Feldpostbriefe von Wehrmachtssoldaten aus der Sowjetunion, 1941–1944* (Wiesbaden: Westdeutscher Verlag, 1998). He notes that only fifteen of these 739 letters mention Jews. Christopher R. Browning, who cites this study, comments: "More research based on private photographic or written sources is needed to arrive at a fuller picture of German perceptions about the East and their change over time" (*The Origins of the Final Solution*, 496n101). In any case, the German soldiers' perception of Jews is clearly antisemitic, judging by the excerpts of some hundred letters supplied by the same Sterz collection, available in the article "'Il n'y a qu'une seule solution pour les juifs: l'extermination.' (There is only one solution for Jews: extermination). L'image du juif dans les lettres de soldats allemands (1939–1944)," *Revue d'histoire de la Shoah* 187 (July–Dec. 2007), 13–58. The title of this article picks up on the title of the book in which these letters first appeared: Walter Manoschek, *"Es gibt nur eines für das Judentum: Vernichtung." Das Judenbild in deutschen Soldatenbriefen, 1939–1944* (Hamburg: Hamburger Edition, 1995).

110. "Befehl des Chefs des Oberkommandos der Wehrmacht über das Verbot, Exekutionen an Sowjetmenschen zu Fotografieren" (Order by the Chief of the Wehrmacht High Command prohibiting photography of executions of Soviet persons), cited in Daniel Uziel and Judith Levin, "Ordinary Men, Extraordinary Photos," *Yad Vashem Studies* 26 (1998): 265–93.

111. "Der Reichsführer-SS hat durch Befehl vom 12.11.1941—Tgb. Nr. I 1481/41 Ads—das Photographieren von Exekutionen verboten und angeordnet, daß, sofern derartige Aufnahmen aus dienstlichen Gründen erforderlich sind, das gesamte Aufnahmematerial archivmäßig zu sammeln ist" (The Reichsführer-SS has by order dated 12/11/1941 . . . prohibited photography of executions and ordered, should such photographs be necessary for reasons of service, that all recorded material be collected for storage in an archive).

112. Ordner Nr. 365 W, Bundesarchiv B 162/30097, Bl. 14. The fact that Heydrich's letter from 16 April 1942 begins with this reference to

an order from Himmler dating back to the previous winter ("Der Reichsführer-SS hat durch Befehl," see previous note) likely explains why this order is often attributed to Heydrich. This is the case in the archive inventories of the USHMM and of Yad Vashem. It is also the case in a footnote in Raul Hilberg's book, *The Destruction of the European Jews* (1:334n181). "On November 12, 1941, Heydrich forbade his own men to take pictures." It was only because Gerhard Schoenberner brought it to my attention that I was able to note the confusion between the two documents, one lost (Himmler), one preserved (Heydrich), in these archive inventories and in the footnote from Hilberg's book.

113. Cited by Annette Krings, *Die Macht der Bilder. Erinnern und Lernen* (Münster: LIT Verlag, 2006), 61.
114. Bundesarchiv, Außenstelle Ludwigsburg, B162/605, Bl. 623. On the subject of these photographs found on dead soldiers, see Hoffmann-Curtius, "Trophäen in Brieftaschen."
115. Johann Gottfried von Herder (1744–1803), *Outlines of a Philosophy for the History of Man* (London: J. Johnson, 1800); digitized edition https://archive.org/details/b22010282/mode/2up, pp. 476–77.
116. Given that Estonia is not, strictly speaking, of "balte" (Baltic) origin, the name *pays baltiques* is sometimes preferred in French when grouping these three countries under a common term. Nonetheless, common usage refers to them, as a whole, as *pays baltes* (Baltic countries).
117. This was the case until the issue of 15 May 1936. Thenceforth, the script was no longer Gothic, but Latin, and the title of the journal, having abandoned the former *Kurzemes Wahrds*, adopted the Latvian spelling *Kurzemes Vārds*. There is nothing arbitrary about this date: it was the moment when dictator Kārlis Ulmanis (1877–1942), who had already dissolved the Parliament and political parties two years earlier, gave himself the title of *Tautas Vadonis* (Nation's Leader), a title which took up the entire breadth of the front page of the *Kurzemes Vārds* on 15 May 1936. *Vadonis* is the Latvian equivalent of *Führer*.
118. Marc Dworzecki, "Histoire des camps nazis en Estonie (1941–1944): L'évolution du système concentrationnaire, la vie quotidienne dans les camps, le non-conformisme et le mouvement de la résistance des déportés" (Tel Aviv, 1967), 56. This 345-page typed document, he says, "contains the gist of the thesis" of its author, defended at the Sorbonne (Paris) in February of that same year. A physician in Vilna before the war, like all the city's surviving Jews, he was confined to the ghetto established in September 1941. Marc Dvorjetski (as his name was then spelled) wrote *Ghetto à l'Est*, translated from the Yiddish by Arnold Mandel (Paris: Robert Marin, 1950). The original title of this work, published two years earlier, picked up

on the nickname that Vilna (now Vilnius) had earned itself through its cultural reach: *Yerushalayim de Litè in kamp un umkum* (Jerusalem-of-Lite in fight and fall). About the expanse in the Ashkenazi world designated by the notion of "Lite," which covered Lithuania, Latvia, Belarus, and Northern Ukraine, see Henri Minczeles, *Vilna, Wilno, Vilnius. la Jérusalem de Lituanie*, preface by Léon Poliakov (Paris: La Découverte, 2000 [1993]).

119. This pact, by which "both High Contracting Parties obligate themselves to desist from any act of violence, any aggressive action, and any attack on each other," was signed in Moscow in Stalin's presence on 23 August 1939 by both the German and the Soviet Ministers of Foreign Affairs, Ribbentrop and Molotov. One month later, on 28 September 1939, its first secret clause was amended in a further protocol, no less secret, and signed by the same ministers, which ruled that "the northern boundary of Lithuania shall represent the boundary of the spheres of influence of Germany and the USSR."

120. Heinz-Ludger Borgert, "Die Kriegsmarine und das Unternehmen 'Barbarossa' am Beispiel des 'Gerichtsbarkeits.' Erlasses und der Ortskommandantur Libau," *Mitteilungen aus dem Bundesarchiv* 1 (1999): 58.

121. The second part (written by Hans-Heinrich Wilhelm) of the book by Helmut Krausnick and Hans-Heinrich Wilhelm, *Die Truppe des Weltanschauungskrieges. Die Einsatzgruppen der Sicherheitspolizei und des SD, 1938–1942* (Stuttgart: Deutsche Verlags-Anstalt, 1981), specifically deals with "Die Einsatzgruppe A der Sicherheitspolizei und des SD 1941/42: Eine exemplarische Studie." Researchers held discussions both about the specific orders that had been given to the Einsatzgruppen and about the date on which these orders were issued. These discussions are illustrated by a sequence of three phases, available in English: first, a review of Krausnick and Wilhelm's book by Albert Streim, who was then director of the Zentralle Stelle der Landesjustizverwaltungen (Central Office of the State Justice Administrations for the Investigation of National Socialist Crimes) in Ludwigsburg; second, Krausnick's response to this review; and third, Streim's reaction to this response. See volumes 4 and 6 of the *Simon Wiesenthal Center Annual*. About the details of the composition of Einsatzgruppe A, see the following note.

122. Large excerpts of Stahlecker's report (Nuremberg, document L-180) were reproduced in 1949 in a collection of documents titled *La Persécution des juifs dans les pays de l'Est présentée à Nuremberg*, published in Paris by Éditions CDJC under the direction of Henri Monneray, a former deputy prosecutor at the Nuremberg Trials (excerpts from the report can be found on pages 279–87 of this collection, with the report on the number of executions on pages 286–87).

Léon Poliakov and Josef Wulf cited certain excerpts of this report in their book *Le IIIe Reich et les Juifs* (Paris: Gallimard, 1959), translated from the German first edition (Berlin: Arani, 1955), 140–48. See also the numerous references to Stahlecker's report in Hilberg's *The Destruction of the European Jews: With a New Postscript by the Author* (New York: Harper & Row, 1973): "All Einsatzgruppen commanders, with the possible exception of the relentless Dr. Stahlecker, realized that the Jews could not be killed in a single sweep" (225). According to the 25 October 1941 report, Einsatzgruppe A was made up of 340 Waffen-SS, 172 motorcycle riders, 350 members of various police corps (uniformed, criminal, auxiliary, and state), 51 interpreters, 35 members of the intelligence agency (SD), 13 "female employees," etc. (p. 292). Stahlecker (b. 1900) was killed in March 1942 during an action against partisans. Heydrich delivered the eulogy at his funeral (see Browning, *The Origins of the Final Solution*, 491n42).

123. "Over the course of summer 1941, in order to make room for wounded German soldiers, security forces would shoot patients in psychiatric facilities across Latvia, particularly in Ielgava [Jelgava], Riga and Dvinsk" (Mayer, *Why Did the Heavens Not Darken?*, 373).

124. About the killings of 30 November and 8 December 1941 near Riga, see below, n145.

125. See Edward Anders and Juris Dubrovskis, "Who Died in the Holocaust? Recovering Names from Official Records," *Holocaust and Genocide Studies* 17, no. 1 (2003): 114–38.

126. See Anders and Dubrovskis, "Who Died in the Holocaust?" and, by the same authors, *Jews in Liepaja, Latvia: A Memorial Book* (Burlingame, CA: Anders Press, 2001).

127. "There are few subjects more difficult than that of this book: the role played by the French state and by a segment of the population between 1940–1944 to subject Jews in France to various legal invalidations, to place a special stamp in their identity documents, and finally, for nearly 76,000 of them, to deliver them over to deportation in the death camps. The emotional charge of this subject in no way justifies the silence on the part of academic historians, to the contrary . . . French readers should not be surprised at the identity of the two authors, the one Canadian and the other American. For our subject is an international one. . . . Racial and ethnic prejudices are not the monopoly of any one country: in this domain, nothing permits anyone to play France's accuser, and vice versa." These are the first lines of the French edition (*Vichy et les juifs* [Paris: Calmann-Lévy, 1981], 11) of Michael R. Marrus and Robert O. Paxton's *Vichy France and the Jews* (Stanford: Stanford University Press, 1995 [1981]).

128. These figures for the June 1941 deportation of Latvian Jews to Siberia—1,771 Jews, that is, 12.2 percent of the 14,194 deported, whereas

Jews made up only 4.79 percent of the overall population—were established in 1995. See Josifs Šteimanis, *History of Latvian Jews*, ed. Edward Anders (Boulder, CO: East European Monographs, 2002), 122n7.

129. "Tuesday June 24 [1941, Bucharest]. In the city, on the walls of the vitrines, two placards of propaganda. . . . The first is of Stalin carrying a white apron stained with blood. The caption: 'The Butcher of Red Square.' The second—captioned 'Who are the Masters of Bolshevism?'—shows a Jew with *tsitsit*, bearded, in a red kaftan, wearing a kippah and holding a sickle with one hand and a hammer with the other. Hidden under the sides of his kaftan are three Soviet soldiers" (Sebastian, *Journal*, 328).

130. The works of various groups from the "History Commission," founded in 1998 on the initiative of Vaira Vike-Freiberga, President of Latvia from 1999 to 2007, deal with "the crimes against humanity . . . between 1940 and 1956." Information about these works is available in English on the website of Latvia's Ministry of Foreign Affairs: https://www.mfa.gov.lv/en/policy/society-integration/history/latvia-s-history-commission.

131. Thus, the "Museum of the Occupation of Latvia," which opened in Riga in 1993, brings together both Occupations—Nazi and Communist—as is indicated by its catalogue, translated into several languages: *Latvia under the Rule of the Soviet Union and National Socialist Germany, 1940–1991* (Riga, 2007). The catalogue addresses the question of collaboration on a single page, according to "the problematic of the 'lesser evil.' For the Jewish population of Latvia, the Soviet occupation is inarguably the lesser evil. The Nazi terror mainly targets them, as a priority. On the contrary, for Latvians, the mechanism of Nazi oppression can seem less brutal than the Communist terror, and collaboration, within the framework of the battle against a still greater evil, Communism, therefore seems more acceptable" (81). In those few lines, one also sees the persistent distinction between "the Jewish population of Latvia" and "Latvians."

132. Andrew Ezergailis, *The Holocaust in Latvia, 1941–1944: The Missing Center* (Riga and Washington, DC: The Historical Institute of Latvia in association with the United States Holocaust Memorial Museum, 1996), xiii. Andrew Ezergailis, born in Latvia in 1931, started teaching history at Ithaca College in New York in 1964. With this book, he published the first truly methodical and archive-based historical inquiry into the genocide of Jews in Latvia. In the preface, in which he states the aims of his project, "to investigate the Latvian guilt in the killing of their countrymen," he briefly mentions his personal implication in the work: "Try as I may, I could not avoid showing my Latvian past and colors." Indeed, there is a certain defensiveness evident at times in Ezergailis's positions, the analysis of

"Latvian guilt" having to deal with the author's own "Latvian past." The fourth cover page of the book quotes excerpts from a review written by Raul Hilberg: "Latvia affords a window to a critical topic, the initiation of the final solution. . . . Ezergailis represents the next wave of Holocaust research: the in-depth exploration of a particular aspect or territory. In that sense he is a pioneer and his work serves as a model."

133. "On a per capita basis, the Latvians, numbering some 1,600,000, were represented as heavily as any nation in the destruction of the Jews. As soon as German forces reached the Latvian capital of Riga on July 1, 1941, volunteers banded together with German approval. Among the entrants into the new auxiliary were officers and soldiers who had served in the army of independent Latvia; soldiers who had been discharged or who had deserted from the 24th (Latvian) Territorial Rifle Corps of the Red Army; former members of the *Aiszargi*, the civil guard, which had been maintained by the prewar Latvian state; members and sympathizers of the Perkonkrust, a right-wing movement that was extreme enough to have been outlawed while Latvia was still independent; university graduates who had belonged to fraternities; athletes and gymnastics teachers; relative of Latvians deported by the Soviets; and assorted youths" (Hilberg, *Perpetrators, Victims, Bystanders*, 99–100).

134. "Antisemitism in Latvia still awaits its historian" (Ezergailis, *The Holocaust in Latvia*, 19). "As the exact number of victims of the Nazi occupation will never be known, neither will the number of people participating in the killings" (Ezergailis, *The Holocaust in Latvia*, 21). Ezergailis's book was published in 1996. As far as the city of Libau [Liepaja] is concerned, in any case, this assertion about the future ("will never be known") would be refuted several years later by Edward Anders's research (see below n146), which established the total number of Jewish victims and the identities of 95 percent of them.

135. "One Year of German Occupation in Latvia," report by Voldemar (Voldemārs) Salnais, in Andrew Ezergailis, ed., *Stockholm Documents, The German Occupation of Latvia, 1941–1945: What Did America Know?* (Riga: Historical Institute of Latvia, 2002), 13, 33.

136. *Kurzemes Vārds*, 2 July 1941. This reference to *vadonim* (*vadonis*), the Latvian equivalent of *Führer*, when joined to Hitler's name, was bound to sound familiar to Latvians since the dictator Kārlis Ulmanis named himself *Tautas Vadonis* (The Nation's Leader) in 1936.

137. *Kurzemes Vārds*, 8 July 1941.

138. About Viktors Arājs and the commando bearing his name that killed more than 20,000 Jews in Latvia, see the chapter "The Arājs Commando" in Ezergailis, *The Holocaust in Latvia*. The author's

at times somewhat defensive position is visible, for instance, in the caption of a 1942 photograph of Viktors Arājs with some of his commando after their return to Latvia from training undertaken at the SD school in Fürstenberg, Germany. In this caption, Ezergailis writes: "Although they wear the black patches of the SD, as yet the men are not dressed in German uniforms. Note the absence of the SS rune insignia" (p. 174). Viktors Arājs was arrested in Germany at the end of the war by the British occupying forces and then released in 1948. He lived in Frankfurt under an assumed name until his arrest in 1975. Sentenced the following year to life in prison by the court of Hamburg, he died in 1986.

139. "Our knowledge of the extermination of the Jews is more complete for Liepaja than for any other Latvian city, except Riga," writes Andrew Ezergailis (*The Holocaust in Latvia*, 305n48). This information, he specifies, comes for the most part from the trial of the Germans responsible for these massacres, which was held at Hannover in 1971.

140. "When the Germans took Libau, the women's prison was used as the site of capture and grouping of all arrested Jews to be killed by shooting" (*Landgericht Hannover, Strafurteil gegen Grauel und andere*, 1970, 2Js291/60, 136).

141. Cited in Borgert, "Die Kriegsmarine," 61.

142. These figures from the 1935 census can be found in Ezergailis, *The Holocaust in Latvia*, 62.

143. Borgert, "Kriegsmarine," 61. Libau naval commandant Hans Kawelmacher (b. 1891) changed his name after the war "on the advice of an official" in the Ministry of the Interior in Bonn to avoid persecution by the Soviets or the East Germans (Borgert, "Kriegsmarine," 65). See also Hans-Heinrich Wilhelm, "'Inventing' the Holocaust in Latvia," in *Bitter Legacy: Confronting the Holocaust in the USSR*, ed. Zvi Gitelman (Bloomington: Indiana University Press, 1997), 120.

144. *Kurzemes Vārds*, 13 December 1941.

145. Dr. Emil (Fritz) Dietrich, *Kriegstagebuch, SS- und Polizeiführer Libau, 20 September 1941–30 November 1943*. This 159-page handwritten document is housed in the National Archives of Latvia as document P83-1-21. After Libau, Dietrich participated in the massacre that took place in the Rumbula forest, ten kilometers from Riga. It was here that, on two days—30 November and 8 December 1941—in six pits that Russian prisoners of war had dug earlier in November, between 1,000 and 1,500 men from various German and Latvian units killed 25,000 men, women, and children, healthy and sick (24,000 Latvian Jews and 1,000 German Jews). The Jews had been transported from the Riga ghetto, where 29,000 Jews then lived. A thousand who refused to go any further were killed either in the ghetto

or along the road leading toward Rumbula. The second day of the massacre—8 December—"was even more gruesome because everyone knew what was going to happen, although the Jews of the ghetto hoped against hope" (Ezergailis, *The Holocaust in Latvia*, 256). The Rumbula massacre was carried out on the orders of the new Higher SS and Police Leader of the Reichskommissariat Ostland, Friedrich Jeckeln, who had just been sent by Himmler to execute in the Ostland what had been carried out two months earlier in the Ukraine, particularly at Babi Yar, where the Germans and Ukrainians of Einsatzkommando C had, also over the course of two days—28–29 September 1941—killed nearly 35,000 people, or half of Kiev's Jewish population. In Rumbula, Fritz Dietrich, commander of a company of the Schutzpolizei's 22nd Battalion, had a specific assignment: the implementation of a machine-gun post. See A. Ezergailis, *The Holocaust in Latvia*, 246. Sentenced to death by a Soviet military tribunal at Riga, Fritz Dietrich (b. 1898) was hanged in October 1948 at Landsberg Prison in Bavaria, the same prison where Hitler had written *Mein Kampf* when he was incarcerated there between 1923 and 1924. Historian Simon Dubnov (Doubnov in French), who was born in 1860 in Belarus, lived in Berlin from 1922 until August 1933, when he left for Riga. This is why he was among the Jews massacred in Rumbula eight years later. Among the editions of his books in French by Éditions du Cerf (with the spelling Doubnov), see *Histoire moderne du peuple juif*, trans. Salomon Jankélévitch, preface by Pierre Vidal-Naquet, 1994, and *Le Livre de ma vie* (see above, n31). In this last book, pages in his diary are quoted in which he is discussing the ongoing completion of his *Histoire moderne du peuple juif*: "May 7. . . . I have a whole series of years in Berlin on the horizon and, in my dreams, the very last years of my life in the calm of Eretz-Israel. It is too late now to go there to work and live, but perhaps, before I die, I will manage to get there to see the sky that inspired my ancestors, my prophets" (*Le Livre de ma vie*, 930). Sebastian wrote: "Monday, September 25, [1939]. . . . Then I read the pages in Dubnov's *Histoire des juifs* on Venice, Padua, Prague, Vienna, and Frankfurt in the 16th century. In reading, I traveled in time. It is good to know one belongs to a people who has seen a great deal of it over the centuries, some of which [was] worse than today" (Sebastian, *Journal*, 211).

146. Born in 1926, Edward Anders is Professor Emeritus of Chemistry at the University of Chicago. Himself a Jewish survivor from Libau, in 1998 he began researching the identities of Jews from his hometown to learn what had happened to them between June 1941 and the end of the war. By critically examining and crosschecking various series of records (including two censuses, one from 1935 and the other from 1941), and through the use of statistical calculations, Anders

and a student of political science in Riga managed to identify more than 95 percent of these victims. See especially Anders and Dubrovskis, "Who Died in the Holocaust?" Other research Anders did on his hometown during the war included editing and publishing the journal that a Jewish schoolteacher from Libau, Kalman Linkimer (1912–88), had kept between 22 June 1941 and 20 February 1945 (with a few interruptions): *Nineteen Months in a Cellar: How 11 Jews Eluded Hitler's Henchmen. The Diary of Kalman Linkimer (1912–1988)*, ed. Edward Anders, trans. Rebecca Margolis (Burlingame, CA: Anders Press, 2011). This journal contains a great deal of specific and detailed information about the successive episodes of persecution and, as concerns eleven of them, the survival of the last Jews of Libau under the occupation.

147. Landgericht Hannover, Strafurteil gegen Grauel und andere, 1970, 2 Js 291/60, Zentralstelle der Landesjustizverwaltungen zur Aufklärung von NS-Verbrechen, Ludwigsburg. The record of this trial was published in its entirety in *Justiz und NS-Verbrechen. Sammlung deutscher Strafurteile wegen nazionalsozialistischer Tötungsverbrechen* 36, no. 760 (Amsterdam/Munich: Amsterdam University Press/K.G. Saur Verlag, 2006), 106–298.

148. Stadtgericht Berlin vom 18.03.1971, 101a Bs 24/70. This trial was published in its entirety in *DDR-Justiz und NS-Verbrechen. Sammlung deutscher Strafurteile wegen Nazionalsozialistischer Tötungsverbrechen* 2, no. 1,046 (Amsterdam/Munich: Amsterdam University Press/K.G. Saur Verlag), 323–52.

149. *Justiz und NS-Verbrechen*, 194.

150. *Justiz und NS-Verbrechen*, 194.

151. *Justiz und NS-Verbrechen*, 195.

152. According to witnesses from the Hannover Trial, this pit was about sixty meters long and four meters wide (*Justiz und Nazi-Verbrechen*, 195). The dimensions Andrew Ezergailis provides in *The Holocaust in Latvia* (294) are approximately one hundred meters by three.

153. The short story "The Shawl," by Cynthia Ozick (born 1928), was first published in the 26 May 1980 issue of *The New Yorker*. See https://www.newyorker.com/magazine/1980/05/26/the-shawl.

154. Stern, *Le Savoir-deporté*, 197–200.

155. Browning, *Ordinary Men*, 73. "*Selbst der Angeklagte schildert das Geschehen als grauenvoll*" (the accused himself depicts the event as horrendous), states the Berlin judgment of Hans Baumgartner, immediately adding that this by no means prevented him from taking part in it on a daily basis (*DDR-justiz und NS-Verbrechen*, 339). We know how much research has been done on these men, ordinary or not, in all kinds of disciplines. Confirming the findings of previous studies or sometimes in total disagreement with them, all of this research is looking for answers to these endless and nagging ques-

tions. On the "banality of evil" (Arendt, *Eichmann in Jerusalem*). On the "authoritarian personality" (Theodor Adorno, *The Authoritarian Personality*). On "obedience to authority" (Stanley Milgram, *Obedience to Authority: An Experimental View*). On "the massive conversion to cruelty" (Zygmunt Bauman, *Modernity and the Holocaust*). On the "psychological conditions conducible to evil" (Robert Jay Lifton, *The Nazi Doctors: Medical Killing and the Psychology of Genocide*). On situations where "volunteering to kill was . . . the norm" (Daniel Jonah Goldhagen, *Hitler's Willing Executioners: Ordinary Germans and the Holocaust*). On the "daily operations" of the killers who "were able to act quickly and efficiently" because "the killing operations were standardized" (Hilberg, *The Destruction of the European Jews*). On the differences between "Zealots, Vulgarians, and Bearers of Burdens" (Hilberg, *Perpetrators, Victims, Bystanders*). On the "heavy stress that these killings imposed upon" the killers (Friedländer, *The Years of Extermination*). On . . . on . . . on . . . Endless and nagging questions, indeed.

156. Before the end of 1941, nearly 40,000 Jews had been killed by the Germans and the Lithuanians of the Einsatzgruppen in Ponary forest, near Vilna (Vilnius). On the subject of these Germans, Marc Dvorjetski wrote: "It was generally men who, at home, were faithful and devoted husbands, tender fathers who gently stroked the hair of their children, charitable and sensitive people who took care not to step on the tail of a cat, who opened the cage for a little bird to set it free. But these same men, when in uniform and receiving orders, were ready to conduct mass killings, to torture the elderly, to beat babies to death, to crack the skulls of small children against tree trunks in the forest, this very forest where they proceed to the mass killings. And even if, once home, they stroke the hair of their own children once again, listen to the warble of the birds once again" (Dvorjetski, *Ghetto à l'Est*, 195). About the author of this work, see above, n118.

157. On the cover of the first edition of Browning's *Ordinary Men*, there is a cropped photograph taken, probably in the fall of 1942, in Luków, east of Warsaw, of three SS men, one of whom is all smiles. The full photograph, reproduced in the photo section between pages 40 and 41, shows them posing for the camera beside two Jewish men in prayer shawls with their arms in the air, one crouching, one kneeling.

158. On this topic, see Carl-Emil Strott's subpoena submission above, pp. 56–59.

159. Stahlecker Report, 15 October 1941. Cited in Hilberg, *The Destruction of the European Jews* 1:319.

160. This six-page report from 2 January 1942, sent from Libau to Riga, is cataloged in the German Federal Archives (Bundesarchiv, Außen-

stelle Ludwigsburg) under the number BArc B 162/19276, Bl. 64a–65.
161. Already on 11 October 1941, the Gebietskommissar of Libau, that is, the local civil authority, notified his superior, the Generalkommissar, of the consternation in the city following the murder of approximately 500 Jews. He added that the mayor, who usually agreed with him in everything, had informed him of his constituents' serious displeasure over the matter (LVVA, P-69-1-17, pp. 124–26; cited in Ezergailis, *The Holocaust in Latvia*, 305n52.
162. *Justiz und NS-Verbrechen*, 195.
163. *Justiz und NS-Verbrechen*, 290.
164. See above, p. 8. The wartime archives make it clear that, after a decade of covering Germany with antisemitic texts and caricatures, the weekly magazine had succeeded in making these depictions the main point of reference. On the back of a photograph of Jewish men evidently looted from a Jewish home in Lublin and sent to the editorial offices of *Der Stürmer*, the sender, a German policeman, writes: "Dear *Stürmer*, this photo tells it all!" See Uziel and Levin, "Ordinary Men, Extraordinary Photos."
165. *Standortbefehl* no. 6, 23 December 1941. A copy of this document is available at the Jewish Museum of Riga.
166. At the Berlin trial (see above, n153), the accused Hans Baumgartner said that he remembered two points with certainty regarding the killings: "*weil es die Fälle waren, wo der SD-Angehörige Str. [Strott] die Erschiessungsaktion fotografierte*" (because these were cases where the SD-affiliated Str. [Strott] photographed the executions by firing squad) (*DDR-Justiz und NS-Verbrechen*, 340). At the Hannover trial, a defendant said that he saw both Strott and another man taking photographs on 15 December 1941 during the executions in which he himself had taken part that day. "Photographs were submitted to the court, which doubtless had been taken during the December action in Shkede and were recognized as such by the witnesses. However, the court was unable to establish that Str. [Strott] had taken these photographs because the witnesses contradicted each other on the subject of the origin of these photos, so that it could not be established with absolute certainty" (*Justiz und Verbrechen*, 227). In both of these volumes, which belong to the records of trials of Nazi criminals initiated by German courts beginning in 1945 (38 volumes published in 2007 for West Germany, *Justiz und NS-Verbrechen*; 9 volumes for East Germany, *DDR-Justiz und NS-Verbrechen*), under the direction of Christiaan F. Rüter and Dick W. de Mildt, the use of shortened names and/or initials is a result of German legislation around the protection of privacy. Full names are only used in these volumes for the accused who were sentenced to death or life imprisonment.

167. The seven pages of Strott's summons are contained in document Bundesarchiv B 162/2627 (pp. 1,659–65).
168. The term used here, translated as "heap," is *Haufen*, which may signify either a bunch as in a pile of objects, or a bunch in the sense of a group of people. The quotation marks the clerk placed around *Haufen* in his transcription of Strott's words makes it rather easy to guess which "heap" Strott was talking about when expressing himself in such a manner.
169. The Allgemeine SS (General SS) was a branch of the SS.
170. *Justiz und NS-Verbrechen*, 234.
171. *Justiz und NS-Verbrechen*, 110.
172. The "Reichskommissariat Ostland" covered, among others, the Baltic States and part of Belarus.
173. Browning, *The Origins of the Final Solution*, 285.
174. Six months later, the protocol of the Wannsee Conference likewise specified that the Jews of the Soviet Union's territory were to be deported eastward *unter Trennung der Geschlechter* (with the sexes separated).
175. LVVA, P-1026-1-3, pp. 237–39. Stahlecker's memorandum of 6 August 1941 is translated into English in Ezergailis, *The Holocaust in Latvia*, 378–80.
176. This correspondence was presented on 17 April 1946 at the Nuremberg Trials of the main Nazi leaders during the cross-examination of Alfred Rosenberg (*Trial of the Major War Criminals before the International Military Tribunal, Nuremberg, 14 November 1945–1 October 1946*), 5:252. Rosenberg was born in 1893 to a German family in Estonia. Editor from 1921 of the *Völkischer Beobachter*, the press organ of the NSDAP, he was the official Party theorist. In 1934, Hitler put him in charge of the "spiritual and philosophical education" of various Nazi organizations (*Das Deutsche Fuehrer Lexikon*, 1934/35, a document presented at the trial). On 17 July 1941, Hitler named him Reichsminister für die besetzten Ostgebiete (Reich Minister for the Occupied Eastern Territories). Sentenced to death at Nuremberg, Rosenberg was hanged in October 1946.
177. This letter is reproduced in facsimile at the permanent exhibition of the House of the Wannsee Conference in Berlin, *Die Wannsee-Konferenz und der Völkermord an den europäischen Juden* (The Wannsee Conference and the Genocide of European Jews) and in the exhibition's catalog, published under the same title in 2006 (on page 90).
178. Hilberg, *The Destruction of the European Jews*, 1:392.
179. This nine-page "Jäger report" from 1 December 1941 is available at https://phdn.org/archives/holocaust-history.org/works/jaeger-report/htm/img001.htm.en.html. After the war, Karl Jäger (b. 1910) lived in hiding under a false identity. Discovered in 1959, he com-

mitted suicide in prison on 22 June of that same year before his trial was held.

180. The number of persons killed at Shkede during the war is not known exactly. Because of coastal erosion in the winter when the wind pushes the sand inward, some bones still with remnants of clothing were exhumed soon after 1945. The number of confirmed deaths was based on the number of recovered skulls, and the bones were collected and interred in a Libau cemetery. This number was included in the total of 8,333 persons found at Shkede (a number determined in 1952), which also included the recovered remains of Latvian soldiers and officers (Liepaja History and Art Museum, Invent no. 6850, 15 July 1952).

181. The perception of what may be a "substantial number" sometimes seems surprising. In his book *Latvia in World War II* (New York: Fordham University Press, 2006), historian Valdis O. Lumans writes that the ghettos of Riga, of Liepaja (Libau), and of another Latvian city, Daugavpils, "still contained substantial numbers of Jews" (p. 247), while specifying on the same page that the Libau ghetto "housed about 800 souls." A "substantial" number, these 800 "souls" still alive in June 1942, who a year earlier were 7,000?

182. Edward Anders (see above, n151) edited and annotated the testimony of a Jew from Liepaja, Solomon Feigerson (b. 1930), who escaped the subsequent stages of the persecution—the arrival of the Germans in his hometown, the massacres of 1941 and 1942, the ghetto, Kaiserwald camp near Riga, and the camp at Stutthof: "The Tragic Fate of Liepaja Jews" (trans. from Russian by Helena Belova, in Anders, ed., *Jews in Liepaja*).

183. Robert and Johanna Sedul. They are among the 138 Latvian recipients of the title "Righteous Among the Nations" between 1966 and 2007. The title is awarded by the Israeli memorial Yad Vashem to non-Jews who, selflessly and at the risk of their freedom or their lives, provided assistance to endangered Jews during the Second World War.

184. I received copies of these photographs, with typed captions on the back, from Gerhard Schoenberner (about him see above, pp. 3–5).

185. About the published text of this trial, see above, n153.

186. About the designation "Copyright: Public Domain," see above, p. 2 and n3.

SELECT BIBLIOGRAPHY

Adorno, Theodor. *The Authoritarian Personality.* New York: Norton, 1969.
Alary, Éric. "Les juifs et la ligne de démarcation. 1940–1943." *Les Cahiers de la Shoah* 5, no. 1 (2001): 13–49.
Améry, Jean. *At the Mind's Limits: Contemplations by a Survivor on Auschwitz and Its Realities.* Translated by Sidney Rosenfeld and Stella P. Rosenfeld. Bloomington: Indiana University Press, 1980.
Anders, Edward, and Juris Dubrovskis. *Jews in Liepaja, Latvia: A Memorial Book.* Burlingame, CA: Anders Press, 2001.
———. "Who Died in the Holocaust? Recovering Names from Official Records." *Holocaust and Genocide Studies* 17, no. 1 (2003): 114–38.
Arad, Yitzhak, ed. *The Pictorial History of the Holocaust.* New York: Macmillan, 1990.
Arendt, Hannah. *Eichmann in Jerusalem: A Report on the Banality of Evil.* Introduction by Amos Elon. New York: Penguin, 2006 [1963].
Baier, Lothar. *Un Allemand né de la dernière guerre. Essai à l'usage des Français.* Afterword by Nadine Fresco. Brussels: Editions Complexe, 1986.
Bartov, Omer. "Guerre barbare. Politique guerrière de l'Allemagne et choix moraux pendant la Seconde Guerre mondiale." *Revue d'histoire de la Shoah* 187 (July–Dec. 2007): 113–42.
Bauman, Zygmunt. *Modernity and the Holocaust.* New York: Cornell University Press, 1992.
Beradt, Charlotte. *Rêver sous le IIIe Reich.* Translated by Pierre Saint-Germain. Foreword by Martine Leibovici. Afterwords by Reinhart Koselleck and François Gantheret. Paris: Payot, 2002.
Blum, Léon. *Du mariage.* Paris: Paul Ollendorff, 1907.
Boitel, Anne. *Le Camp de Rivesaltes 1941–1942. Du centre d'hébergement au "Drancy de la zone libre."* Preface by Michel Cadé. Afterword by Serge Klarsfeld. Perpignan: Presses Universitaires de Perpignan, 2001.
Borgert, Heinz-Ludger. "Die Kriegsmarine und das Unternehmen 'Barbarossa' am Beispiel des 'Gerichtsbarkeits.' Erlasses und der Ortskommandantur Libau." *Mitteilungen aus dem Bundesarchiv* 1 (1999): 52–64.

Brecht, Bertold. *Die Gedichte*. Edited by Jan Knopf. Frankfurt: Suhrkamp Editions, 2007.

Browning, Christopher R. *Ordinary Men: Reserve Police Battalion 101 and the Final Solution in Poland*. New York: Harper Perennial, 1998.

Browning, Christopher R., with contributions by Jürgen Matthäus. *The Origins of the Final Solution: The Evolution of Nazi Jewish Policy, September 1939–March 1942*. Lincoln: University of Nebraska Press, 2004.

Burrin, Philippe. *La France à l'heure allemande. 1940–1944*. Paris: Éditions du Seuil, 1995.

Cayrol, Jean. *Poèmes de la nuit et du brouillard*. Paris: Pierre Seghers, 1946.

Celan, Paul. "Speech on the Occasion of Receiving the Literature Prize of the Free Hanseatic City of Bremen [26 January 1958]." In *Selected Poems and Prose of Paul Celan*. Translated by John Felstiner. New York: W. W. Norton, 2001.

Celan, Paul, and Gisèle Celan-Lestrange. *Correspondance (1951–1970)*, edited and annotated by Bernard Badiou. 2 vols. Paris: Éditions du Seuil, 2001.

Celan, Paul, and Ilana Shmueli. *Correspondance (1965–1970)*, edited by Ilana Shmueli and Thomas Sparr. Translated and edited by Bertrand Badiou. Paris: Éditions du Seuil, 2006.

Dagen, Philippe. "Des photographies de propagande nazie provoquent un malaise." *Le Monde* (Paris), 12 April 2008.

Doubnov, Simon [Semyen Dubnov]. *Le Livre de ma vie. Souvenirs et réflexions. Matériaux pour l'histoire de mon temps*. Translated and annotated by Brigitte Bernheimer. Preface by Henri Minczeles. Paris: Éditions du Cerf, 2001.

Dvorjetski (Dworzecki), Marc. *Ghetto à l'Est*. Translated by Arnold Mandel. Paris: Robert Marin, 1950.

——. "Histoire des camps nazis en Estonie (1941–1944). L'évolution du système concentrationnaire, la vie quotidienne dans les camps, le non-conformisme et le mouvement de la résistance des deportés." Unpublished manuscript. Tel Aviv, 1967.

Ezergailis, Andrew. *The Holocaust in Latvia, 1941–1944: The Missing Center*. Riga and Washington, DC: The Historical Institute of Latvia in association with the United States Holocaust Memorial Museum, 1996.

——, ed. *Stockholm Documents, The German Occupation of Latvia, 1941–1945: What Did America Know?* Riga: The Historical Institute of Latvia, 2002.

Friedländer, Saul. *Nazi Germany and the Jews*, vol. 1: *The Years of Persecution 1933–1939*. New York: Harper Perennial, 1998.

——. *Nazi Germany and the Jews*, vol. 2: *The Years of Extermination 1939–1945*. New York: HarperCollins, 2007.

Goldhagen, Daniel Jonah. *Hitler's Willing Executioners: Ordinary Germans and the Holocaust*. London: Abacus, 2008.
Gouri, Haïm. *Facing the Glass Booth: The Jerusalem Trial of Adolf Eichmann*. Translated by Michael Swirsky. Detroit: Wayne State University Press, 2004.
Grynberg, Anne. *Les Camps de la honte. Les internés juifs des camps français, 1939–1944*. Paris: La Découverte, 1999.
Heer, Hannes. "Das Haupt der Medusa. Die Verbrechen der Wehrmacht und der Kampf um die Erinnerung in Deutschland." *Geschichte und Region/Storia e regione* 16, no. 2 (2007): 193–94.
Henriot, Philippe, ed. Foreword to *Carnets secrets de Jean Zay*, Paris: Les Éditions de France, 1942.
Herder, Johann Gottfried. *Outlines of a Philosophy for the History of Man*. London: J. Johnson, 1800.
Hesse, Klaus, and Philipp Springer. *Vor aller Augen. Fotodokumente des nationalsozialistischen Terrors in der Provinz*, edited by Reinhard Rürup. Essen: Klartext Verlag, 2002.
Hilberg, Raul. *The Destruction of the European Jews*. 3rd ed. New Haven: Yale University Press, 2003 [1961].
———. *Perpetrators, Victims, Bystanders: The Jewish Catastrophe 1933–1945*. New York: Harper Perennial, 1993.
Hoffmann-Curtius, Kathrin. "Trophäen in Brieftaschen: Fotografien von Wehrmachts-, SS- und Polizei-Verbrechen." Kunsttexte.de, March 2002, available at https://docplayer.org/17128503-Trophaeen-in-brieftaschen-fotografien-von-wehrmachts-ss-und-polizei-verbrechen.html.
Höss, Rudolf. *Commandant of Auschwitz*. Translated by Constantine FitzGibbon. Introduction by Primo Levi. London: Phoenix Press, 2000.
Humburg, Martin. *Das Gesicht des Krieges. Feldpostbriefe von Wehrmachtssoldaten aus der Sowjetunion, 1941–1944*. Wiesbaden: Westdeutscher Verlag, 1998.
Hüppauf, Bernd. "Emptying the Gaze: Framing Violence through the Viewfinder." In *War of Extermination: The German Military in World War II, 1941–1944*, edited by Hannes Heer and Klaus Neumann, 345–77. New York: Berghahn Books, 2000.
———. "'Il n'y a qu'une seule solution pour les juifs: l'extermination.' L'image du juif dans les lettres de soldats allemands (1939–1944)," edited and prefaced by Walter Manoschek. Translated from German by Jean Ruffet. *Revue d'histoire de la Shoah* 187 (July–Dec. 2007): 13–58.
Klabund (Alfred Henschke). *Die Harfenjule. Neue Zeit-, Streit- und Leidgeschichte*. Berlin: Die Schmiede, 1927.
Klarsfeld, Serge. *Le Calendrier de la persécution des juifs en France, 1940–1944*. Paris: FFDJF & The Beate Klarsfeld Foundation, 1993.
Klee, Ernst, Willi Dressen, and Volker Riess, eds. *"The Good Old Days": The Holocaust as Seen by Its Perpetrators and Bystanders*. Translated

by Deborah Burstone. Foreword by Hugh Trevor-Roper. Old Saybrook, CT: Konecky & Konecky, 1996.
Klemperer, Victor. *Geschichte der französischen Literatur im 18. Jahrhundert.* Tübingen: Max Niemeyer Verlag, 1954.
———. *I Shall Bear Witness: The Diaries of Victor Klemperer (1933–1941).* Translated by Martin Chalmers. London: Weidenfeld and Nicolson, 1998.
———. *To the Bitter End: The Diaries of Victor Klemperer (1942–1945).* Translated by Martin Chalmers. London: Weidenfeld and Nicolson, 1999.
———. *The Language of the Third Reich: LTI. Lingua Tertii Imperii.* Translated by Martin Brady. London: Bloomsbury, 2000.
———. *The Lesser Evil: The Diaries of Victor Klemperer (1945–1959).* Translated by Martin Chalmers. London: Weidenfeld and Nicolson, 2003.
Krausnick, Helmut, and Hans-Heinrich Wilhelm. *Die Truppe des Weltanschauungskrieges. Die Einsatzgruppen der Sicherheitspolizei und des SD, 1938–1942.* Stuttgart: Deutsche Verlags-Anstalt, 1981.
Krings, Annette. *Die Macht der Bilder. Erinnern und Lernen.* Münster: LIT Verlag, 2006.
Laharie, Claude. *Le camp de Gurs, 1939–1945. Un aspect méconnu de l'histoire de Vichy.* Preface by Artur London. Pau: J&D Éditions, 1993.
Lanzmann, Claude. *Shoah.* Preface by Simone de Beauvoir. Paris: Gallimard, series *Folio*, 2001 [1985].
Laqueur, Walter. *The Terrible Secret: Suppression of the Truth about Hitler's Final Solution.* Boston: Little, Brown and Company, 1980.
Laval, Michel. *Brasillach ou la trahison du clerc.* Paris: Hachette, 1992.
Levi, Primo. *The Drowned and the Saved.* Translated by Raymond Rosenthal. New York: Random House, 1988.
Lifton, Robert Jay. *The Nazi Doctors: Medical Killing and the Psychology of Genocide.* New York: Basic Books, 2017.
Lindeperg, Sylvie. *"Nuit et brouillard." Un film dans l'histoire.* Paris: Odile Jacob, 2007.
Linkimer, Kalman. *Nineteen Months in a Cellar: How 11 Jews Eluded Hitler's Henchmen. The Diary of Kalman Linkimer (1912–1988),* edited by Edward Anders. Translated by Rebecca Margolis. Burlingame, CA: Anders Press, 2011.
Loubes, Olivier. "D'un drapeau l'autre. Jean Zay (1914–1940)." *Vingtième Siècle. Revue d'histoire* 71 (2001): 37–51.
Lumans, Valdis O. *Latvia in World War II.* New York: Fordham University Press, 2006.
Mann, Thomas. *Order of the Day: Political Essays and Speeches of Two Decades.* New York: Alfred A. Knopf, 1942.
Manoschek, Walter. *"Es gibt nur eines für das Judentum: Vernichtung."*

SELECT BIBLIOGRAPHY

Das Judenbild in deutschen Soldatenbriefen, 1939–1944. Hamburg: Hamburger Edition, 1995.

Marrus, Michael R., and Robert O. Paxton. *Vichy et les juifs*. Paris: Calmann-Lévy, 1981.

———. *Vichy France and the Jews*. Stanford: Stanford University Press, 1995 [1981].

Mayer, Arno J. *Why Did the Heavens Not Darken? The "Final Solution" in History*. New York: Pantheon, 1988.

Milgram, Stanley. *Obedience to Authority: An Experimental View*. London: Printer and Martin, 2005.

Milton, Sybil. "The Camera as Weapon: Documentary Photography and the Holocaust." *Holocaust and Genocide Studies* 1, no. 1 (1986): 27–61.

———. "Photography as Evidence of the Holocaust." *History of Photography* 23, no. 4 (1999): 303–12.

Minczeles, Henri. *Vilna, Wilno, Vilnius. La Jérusalem de Lituanie*. Preface by Léon Poliakov. Paris: La Découverte, 2000 [1993].

Monneray, Henri. *La Persécution des juifs dans les pays de l'Est présentée à Nuremberg*. Paris: Éditions CDJC, 1949.

Noiriel, Gérard. *Immigration, antisémitisme et racisme en France (XIXe–XXe siècle). Discours publics, humiliations privées*. Paris: Fayard, 2007.

Novodorsqui-Deniau, Monique. *Pithiviers-Auschwitz. 17 juillet 1942, 6h15*, edited by Katy Hazan, Benoît Verny, and Nadine Fresco. Preface by Simone Veil. Orléans: Éditions Cercil, 2006.

Poliakov, Léon, and Josef Wulf. *Das dritte Reich und die Juden*. Berlin: Arani, 1955.

———. *Le IIIe Reich et les Juifs*. Paris: Gallimard, 1959.

Rousso, Henry. *Pétain et la fin de la collaboration. Sigmaringen 1944–1945*. Brussels: Complexe, 1984.

Rüter, C. F., and D. W. de Mildt, eds. *Justiz und NS-Verbrechen. Sammlung deutscher Strafurteile wegen nationalsozialistischer Tötungsverbrechen*, vol. 36, no. 760. Amsterdam: Amsterdam University Press, 2006.

———. *DDR-Justiz und NS-Verbrechen. Sammlung deutscher Strafurteile wegen nationalsozialistischer Tötungsverbrechen*, vol. 2, no. 1046. Amsterdam: Amsterdam University Press, 2013.

Schneider, Gertrude. *Muted Voices: Jewish Survivors of Latvia Remember*. New York: Philosophical Library, 1987.

———. *The Unfinished Road: Jewish Survivors of Latvia Look Back*. New York: Praeger, 1991.

———. *Journey into Terror: Story of the Riga Ghetto*. Westport, CT: Praeger, 2001.

———. *Reise in den Tod. Deutsche Juden in Riga, 1941–1944*. Berlin: Hentrich, 2006.

Schoenberner, Franz. *Confessions of a European Intellectual.* New York: Macmillan, 1946.
———. *Bekenntnisse eines europäischen Intellektuellen.* Munich: Kreisselmeier Verlag, 1964.
Schoenberner, Gerhard. *Der gelbe Stern. Die Judenverfolgung in Europa, 1933 bis 1945.* Hamburg: Argument Verlag, 2013 [1960].
———. *L'Étoile jaune. Le génocide juif en Europe, 1933–1945.* Paris: Presses de la Cité, 1982.
———. *The Yellow Star: The Persecution of the Jews in Europe, 1933–1945.* New York: Fordham University Press, 2004.
Sebastian, Mihail. *Journal, 1935–1944.* Translated by Alain Paruit. Preface by Edgar Reichmann. Paris: Stock, 2007.
Šteimanis, Josifs. *History of Latvian Jews,* edited by Edward Anders. Boulder, CO: East European Monographs, 2002.
Stern, Anne-Lise. *Le Savoir-déporté. Camps, histoire, psychanalyse,* edited and foreword by Nadine Fresco and Martine Leibovici. Paris: Éditions du Seuil, series *Points-Essais,* 2007 [2004].
Teschner, Gerhard J. *Die Deportation der badischen und saarpfälzischen Juden am 22. Oktober 1940.* Frankfurt: Peter Lang Verlag, 2002.
Thion, Serge. *Vérité historique ou vérité politique? Le dossier de l'affaire Faurisson. La question des chambres à gaz.* Paris: La Vieille Taupe, 1980.
Uziel, Daniel. "Wehrmacht Propaganda Troops and the Jews." Translated by William Templer. *Yad Vashem Studies* 29 (2001): 27–65.
Uziel, Daniel, and Judith Levin. "Ordinary Men, Extraordinary Photos." *Yad Vashem Studies* 26 (1998): 265–93. Available at https://www.yadvashem.org/articles/academic/ordinary-men-extraordinary-photos.html.
Vernant, Jean-Pierre. *The Universe, the Gods, and Men.* Translated by Lisa Asher. New York: Harper Perennial, 2002.
Weill, Joseph. *Contribution à l'histoire des camps d'internement dans l'Anti-France.* Paris: CDJC, Éd. du Centre, 1946.
Wilhelm, Hans-Heinrich. "'Inventing' the Holocaust in Latvia." In *Bitter Legacy: Confronting the Holocaust in the USSR,* edited by Zvi Gitelman. Bloomington: Indiana University Press, 1997.
Williamson, Gordon. *Die SS. Hitlers Instrument der Macht. Die Geschichte der SS, von der Schutztaffel bis zur Waffen-SS.* Munich: Kaiser Verlag, 2003.
Wyman, David S. *The Abandonment of the Jews: America and the Holocaust, 1941–1945.* New York: Pantheon Books, 1984.

www.ingramcontent.com/pod-product-compliance
Lightning Source LLC
Chambersburg PA
CBHW070046120526
44589CB00035B/2331